Praise for Todd Swift

Todd Swift is the Orson Welles of con[temporary poe]tic, mischievous, irrepressible. This Selec[ted showcases his] gifts; it is sure to win for him a host c[...]
—Mark Ford

There's a completion, a dire prophecy seemingly come true, in Todd Swift's The Ministry of Emergency Situations: Selected Poems. *The brief, incisive first poem, "Shape", sees how the body forms and limits: "Our shape shapes us // ...like entrails / ...the curse." Poems at the end, from Swift's powerful recent volume* When All My Disappointments Came at Once, *grapple with the discovery of a devastating bodily shaping: infertility. Between are riches in manifold registers—lyrics, narratives, eruptions of wit, tributes to ideas and writers and moments, narratives—all full of restless rhythms, creative diction, and a mastery of technique, especially impressive in the many poems which bring new sounds to the tradition of rhyme and meter. The book finally is an account of the unfinished overcoming of the limits it finds all around and within us. Music may have lied in promising the eternal, as Swift remarks in "Mix Tapes". But he creates a music of language in which nature can perhaps be what we say it is, because the seeming permanence of a tree watched throughout a day "suggests to me a kind of love" ("Natural Curve").*
— A.F. Moritz

Todd Swift wears his erudition lightly, even playfully, particularly in his deft use of form and rhyme, and in the sly, insightful way he combines allusions to popular culture and classical tales. But of equal importance to the considerable technique deployed here is the poet's tenderhearted, searchingly ethical voice. Swift displays an acute, sometimes painful sensitivity to the world—as in the marvelous "The Influence of Anxiety at the Seaside with Tea"—as he records the precise details that reveal our virtues and our flaws, or in other words, make us human. This collection, spanning three decades, should solidify this fine poet's international reputation.
—Rose Solari

Readers will delight in reading The Ministry of Emergency Situations, *Todd Swift's Selected Poems. Here is a poet growing every year more surely into his own: his poems are becoming more lyrical, more sure-footed, and more wry in their insights and descriptions. These are learned, interesting poems in a breathtaking variety of forms and modes.*
—Patricia Clark

The Ministry of Emergency Situations

Selected Poems

Todd Swift

MARICK PRESS

LIBRARY OF CONGRESS CATALOGUING
IN PUBLICATION DATA
Swift, Todd
Poems. Selected Poems. English.
The Ministry of Emergency Situations/Todd Swift
ISBN: 978-1-934851-52-4

Copyright © 2014 by Todd Swift

Design and typesetting by HSDesigns
Cover design by HSDesigns

Cover image: *Soldier and Girl at Station,* Alex Colville *(1953)*
glazed tempera
40.6 x 61 cm (16 x 24 in.)
ART GALLERY OF ONTARIO
The Thomson Collection © Art Gallery of Ontario
AGOID.103990
Permission to reproduce is granted by the AGO,
and Ms Ann Kitz, for the Colville Estate.

Printed and bound in the United States.

Marick Press
P.O. Box 36253
Grosse Pointe Farms
Michigan 48236
www.marickpress.com

Distributed by spdbooks.org and Ingram

MARICK PRESS

For my mother Margaret, brother Jordan, sister-in-law Jacinthe and godson, Alex; and my wife, Sara.

Contents

Shape   15
The Cry at Deep Cut   16
Looks   17
Goethe in a Balloon   18
A Solemn Meditation on the Fantastic Four   19
Honk Your Horn if You Are Paranoid   21
A Sonnet for the Lobster Diners   23
The White Kitchen   24
Why I Do Not Carry a Gun   25
Curing   26
Emily Donne   27
Vuillard's Leopards   28
Julian   29
The Lament of Thomas Stearns   30
The Landlord Hate   31
Gun Crazy   32
Evening on Putney Avenue   34
Mary Veronica Swift, 1914–1991   36
Ways of Counting   37
Kanada Post   38
Letting Go   39
Hull Losses   40
Intergalactic Travel   41

The Child, the Family, and the Outside World   43
Trick   44
In My Father's Briefcase   45
Hume Knoll   46
Last Year's Model   47
The New Fedora   48
Water, Running   49
Seven Eights Are Fifty-six   50
After Hardy   52
The Last Days of St Lambert   53
The More Deserved   54
Penthouse Revisited   55
Visiting Westmount   57
The Seven Wonders of the World   60
Rue du Regard   62
The Golden Age of Travel   63
By the Pool   65
On His Wedding   67
Cinéma du Look   68
Homage to Charlotte Rampling   69
Marylebone   70
Be It Resolved That   71
The Tenant of Wildfell Hall   73
On the Back of the Book   74
The Influence of Anxiety
    at the Seaside with Tea   75
Ballad of the Solitary Diner   76
O Magnum Mysterium   78
Tomsk   79
Gentlemen of Nerve   79
Emperor   81
I'm in Love with a German Film Star   85
Modest Proposal   86
Mix Tapes   88

Woman at a Station   89
The Expedition   91
My Universities   92
Natural Curve   93
Communal Garden   94
The Last Blizzard   95
Winter Work in April   97
Riverside Drive   98
The Wedding Photographer   99
I Empty My Wallet   100
The Mountain Lion   102
The Recording Artist   103
Action Comics   104
The Man Who Killed Houdini   105
Writing   106
Envoi   107
Hydra   108
The Mosquito and the Map   109
The Shape of Things to Come   110
The Ministry of Emergency Situations   111
The Oil and Gas University   112
Winter Winter Tennis   113
Taking Tea with Charles Bernstein   114
The Red Bathing Cap   116
"There is, in it"   118
Seaway   119
Trees   120
"Ivo," Marianopolis, 1984   121
Spider-Man 2   122
Library Going   123
The Talking Cure   126
French Poem   127
Mainstream Love Hotel   128
New Theology   129

Green Girl in Vermont   130
Now the Rain's My Only Reader   132
"God has left us like a girl"   134
Canadian Fiction   135
These Days   138
Late History   139
The Teetotaller's Song   140
Skylon   141
The Quest of the Holy Grail   142
War Poetry   143
It's Not a Poem Unless It's Seen   144
Glassco in Quebec
   (Huysmans in France, Brummell in England)   146
Michael Kohlhaas   148
Fertility   151
When All My Disappointments Came at Once   152
Azoospermia   153
Sonnet   155
Slieve Donard   156
The Polish Builders in Hammersmith   158
Shop-worn   160
Hunting Party   161
"Somewhere the mimetic
   is having more fun than I am"   162
"Down From St John's Wood"   163
31 Richford Street, June,
   After Reading Goodland   164
Near St Ives   166
Hope, Maida Vale   167
Slieve Donard II   168
Start Again   170
The Safe Years   172
I go out in my suit, too white for this weather   174
After riding the escalator back   176

St Peter and St Paul   178
Christmas Morning   180
Sea Level at Midnight   181
Presentation   183
Jean Talon, Intendant of New France,
  to the King (1666)   184
On the Joys and Sorrows   186
April Snow   188
Bing Crosby   190
For the Boy in the Choir with Tourette's   192
My wife's organ donor card arrives   193
As "Heavenly Bodies" by Tamaryn Played   194
The Language of the Fan   195
Disorders of Personality   196
I Think of Delmore Schwartz,
  Beside My Sleeping Love   197
The Ailment   200
After the boy band incident   201
The Fourth King   203
Unfinished Study of a French Girl   204
On Learning His Godson
  Has The "Language Gene" Defect FoxP2   206
The Best I Can Do   208
In Memoriam, Seamus Heaney   210
The Book of Platitudes   211

Acknowledgements
About the Book

Shape

Our shape shapes us
our body holds us
to our word and worse.
It is what we cast, what we cut,
how drapes drape us, folds fall
that tells out like entrails
of it all, the curse.
It is not the coin that sets its bank
but the coin that is settled and shut by the purse.

The Cry at Deep Cut

The cry at the first very deep cut that bleeds
is not for the pain or swooping blood
is more for the outrage, the single affront
that we can pour forth
are harmable
may die.

I was most shocked when the blade jumped back in
by my critical eye
I didn't prefer its improvement on my white thumb
though at other times I have been well aware
that the best skin is that laid bare.

Looks

One cannot help another's look,
one's fine features shall not spread
to the other as dry twigs ganging would
under the tyranny of the match.

This is a shame as I understand them,
for the way at the table we talked
was uneasy in her beauty, in my inequality.
Too bad her looks could not to me extend
like the tea she spilled near the end.

Goethe in a Balloon

Greatly excited
by the prospect of expanding
his horizons, Goethe
is said to have one day
hired the first air balloon
to ever successfully soar
above the church bells,

whereupon he peered down
upon his tiny city, and was filled
with a redoubled sense of Man's place
in the universal scheme of things.
Meanwhile, the poor inventor
who had built the craft crouched
terrified over the plans, aware

of a serious flaw in his original
computations, not daring
to disturb the Genius's reverie
and horrified, lest he be the cause
of Europe's finest mind toppling
to the ground, like some ludicrous
Icarus, or demonic basket case.

Looks

One cannot help another's look,
one's fine features shall not spread
to the other as dry twigs ganging would
under the tyranny of the match.

This is a shame as I understand them,
for the way at the table we talked
was uneasy in her beauty, in my inequality.
Too bad her looks could not to me extend
like the tea she spilled near the end.

Goethe in a Balloon

Greatly excited
by the prospect of expanding
his horizons, Goethe
is said to have one day
hired the first air balloon
to ever successfully soar
above the church bells,

whereupon he peered down
upon his tiny city, and was filled
with a redoubled sense of Man's place
in the universal scheme of things.
Meanwhile, the poor inventor
who had built the craft crouched
terrified over the plans, aware

of a serious flaw in his original
computations, not daring
to disturb the Genius's reverie
and horrified, lest he be the cause
of Europe's finest mind toppling
to the ground, like some ludicrous
Icarus, or demonic basket case.

A Solemn Meditation on the Fantastic Four

Gamma Rays pierced them, they returned heroic
though not without difficulties. When all changes,
much remains, but different, even unfortunately
strange, and powerful, so that men point in streets,

their hats tumbling off, and women drop groceries,
to see Galactus, or his herald, in bubbles of concrete,
atoms in galaxies in Manhattan, thrown for a challenge,
and earth-shattering conclusions left monthly, balanced

by the sheer crazy threats of barely thwarted annihilation
and what being super frames. It's clobbering time, yet
not all matters can be solved with orange-granite fists,
limbs that stretch like gum, a molten body of a boy,

or a girl whose fields are clear as glass but cannot yield
their molecular force. Because human, we love as well
as when, to war, we put our armour on, and fend for Troy
or Helen; each wall that's a breakthrough for one army

is another's black hole, defeat whorling in like vacuum
and nothing left save rubble, weakness and air half-fire,
and the rumour of more ruin on the way, the next landing:
the world a place to be conquered by a Silver Surfer, or

a Submariner, blowing what belongs to Triton, Hudson
roiling at the emergence of an aquamarine attack, noble
in its grand indifference to the mere lunged New Yorkers,
abashed but inured to wanton villains and their grandiosity

now that the Baxter Building is the Ur-magnet for wild evil.
Yet, how can Mr Fantastic knowingly enter the fragile
space of his own beloved, without a shameful thought,
that what simple anatomy has wrought, his husbandry

may undo, with his newfound abilities, pure expansion?
Obscenity is no part of the vows that bind a man to spouse
but in the broken house that is radiation's special curse,
who can argue for his long-legged will to stay, just so?

And who may know the proper measure of Ben Grimm's
agony: mightier than a slaughterhouse of oxen, still stone
on stone, and tangerine, his hands a clear sign of clumsy
cold, no subtle fingers here, a demolition of thumbs, a face

like a wrecking ball, and all the passion of a normal man?
Might he not want to break down, be regular now, and take
the blind girl in his athlete's arms, again, no pressure to tackle
Victor Von Doom? Consider the Invisible Girl, later Woman,

whose grace is to go unnoticed, who can keep the rain off
with a shrug of atoms, does she want her genius long or short?
Maybe after a homely battle, she may turn her back and leave
her powers on, so no marriage can reach, no matter the arms

that struggle to strain and pound at her inviolable places?
For Johnny Storm, no tonnage of car wax or peroxide obscures
his film idol's grin eats only oxygen and spits lewd fire, his trim
physique a mitochondrion's macrocosm gone supernova. Sure,

he's beauty jetting from a flame-thrower, a solar rose, flight
hotly incarnate, a stream of fuel lit and flown across the sky,
lean muscle in a tight blue uniform that accepts the burn;
but this, and less. He cannot lift his playmates to the sun

as he may go, but must return too soon with lovers to the ground.
They've found, all four, each as fantastic as a bestiary's apocrypha,
an access to the null and void of life, where Midas fondled yellow.

Honk Your Horn If You Are Paranoid

I am becoming afraid of everything.
This is not a good situation.
Everything is what supports the world.
But suppose it should let go?
I am. Holding everything in perspective
is a tiring spectator sport, the reality

is that when you begin to lose it, big time,
you are already there, lost. Back
is a long way forward, something like
eating a bowl of spiders to overcome
a fear of webs. Not very pleasant,
frankly. Once, my principal came back

from Africa when I was ten, with some
chocolate-covered locusts, and offered them
to my class, sitting on the floor like little Indians;
we ate them, but not me. I was too suspicious then,
as I am now, of such weird delicacies from men.
The world involves a series of plane crashes,

and beautiful women taller than myself. One
of them is my girlfriend. Suppose she was
to offer herself to me, all covered in locusts,
would I eat her sweet tasty bits, or run for cover?
When you turn off a light at night, who says
it will come on in the morning? Not General

Electric. Not even such a gifted multinational
can promise us such permanent illumination.
They know, the suits in their great towers, the world
is all about uncertainty, of that they are certain;
the stock market plunges and spumes free like a dolphin
on that safe basis. There is safety in numbers. Not

all of us will die in the next fiery Boeing lunge
in Chicago or Bombay. Some of us will stay up
to catch the report, shaking our heads before going
to bed, turning out the hall light on the way, musing
that could have been me flying to Jakarta, if only
I had an oil refinery there, that might have been me.

Usually, we slip in baths or fall down weak-limbed ladders,
or stick pulsing, fluid fingers into the wrong sockets,
on-the-job victims of tables and lists, the certainty
that something is coming loose somewhere in the multitudes,
somewhere a boy is loading his AK-47, precisely
to kill your family, your loved ones, everything you see.

A Sonnet for the Lobster Diners

Nothing is pretty about a lobster
you can't tear out; the shell's a wreck
of red and claw, someone's idea
of nasty art exploded on the ocean floor;
but the meat is something else,
the sweet soft promise finally come,
when hot butter's delivery slides along
the fingers and the tongue: a story
with an ending twice as happy as the start;
so all the art of eating out the creature
is to take apart the structure like an act
of war, to get to the armistice beneath
the armour: the white tangy peace of flesh
that pulls as it parts with its own brother.

The White Kitchen

Yes, you are gone
and I believe that bodies rot
when buried in the ground,

though as to what happens
to living creatures
that walk their peripheries

in a distant town
I am helpless to say.
Not dead then, but distant.

On the occult telephone
your voice sounds
as oddly rushed as from the ether,

summoned by a crone.
I can add nothing new
to metaphysical conjecture,

I am no oiled and bound Egyptian,
have no name for what's been done
here in your absence's white kitchen.

Why I Do Not Carry a Gun

It fits perfectly
into a mouth.

It contains bullets.

It is the colour
of dark leather.

It is the length
of a cock.

Because, crouching
on one leg, it can
eliminate a room
of persons. Immediately.

It can be easily concealed.

Because it feels good
in the hand.

Because I would stroke
your cheek gently
with it, often.

Because I want to.

CURING

I have discovered a cure for blindness. It involves glass. You must crush it like you were churning butter. Spread the grains upon a kerchief, stolen from a peasant girl in the fields. Strip naked. This must be done three weeks before harvest (the moon removed) when the sky is the colour of veins under an old woman's skirt. Begin to dance as if dogs were after you. Smear the shards across your genitals like jam. Whimper like the wind worrying for the damned. Be careful to bleed against a wall where recently two lovers have been; gently. Move away from the spot, appearing ashamed. Bind your wounds with splinters. Apply broken eggshells lightly to the open, wandering eyes. In the morning, all is changed: they will not stray again. When you return the kerchief, she will thank you, smiling. Look indirectly at her now. You are in the sun.

Emily Donne

1.

My mistress
carries a flea with her

hops right off the page.

2.

She treats her book like linen,
creased when she's done.

3.

Her eye is never finished
forming of a world,
delicate
as Qs.

4.

She keeps it by the bed,
to warm beneath the cover

every itch
that takes a bite
informs her
of her lover.

5.

In every age
the creature goes

one to another.

Vuillard's Leopards

Remember those paintings by Vuillard,
the ones spotted yellow and brown
in the background like a leopard?
That was wallpaper, my favourite scene.

If legal, I could stroll
right up and take them down
to my room, to have at times
to touch heightened softness, creviced silk,

able to unravel like petals and become screens
a white geisha might come out from silently,
a woman whose materials have forgotten how to rustle
in motion made across, and through, rooms.

Julian

Julian has a hat that is passed down
from his father and it is indestructible.

He gave it to me for the duration of his visit,
four nights and three days,

and I wore it constantly, pretending
to be him. His instructions were simple

in the extreme: not to care for it,
not to protect it from the elements,

for the way of caution leads to weakness,
and the wearer would ruin the quality of the worn.

Instead, he urged me to carry it in to the shower
in the mornings, and crumple it

strongly in the hand, throwing it across the room
with disdain. It lasted my attempts

to destroy its casual form, its legitimate brim.
When he left he promised he would send me one of my own

in about eight to ten weeks. It never came.
I intend to carry my bare head around in similar fashion.

The Lament of Thomas Stearns

I caught a fly this morning
taking its constitutional
across my bare wrist, domed
it under a teacup.
The perfect china shook.
I went upstairs to shave.
The razor held a special status
in my thoughts, bare bodkin
in the bath water. Downstairs
again exactly an hour later
by the cuckoo clock, still
a wild penitent insisted on outlet.
No air soon would give it notice,
the table setting calmed.

All my life I have wanted
to take my fist down,
right onto glass. Begin
a violent process, send birds
scuttling off the near branch.
That would be an event.
Like all the island curled under ash,
bodies with no motion, burnt dolls
in a crusted house, the lava flat
and sullen now that the fire's done,
cold as a widow's night-cap.
Instead, I created a second life
for the creature, tilted an inch
of rim to aperture flight.

Julian

Julian has a hat that is passed down
from his father and it is indestructible.

He gave it to me for the duration of his visit,
four nights and three days,

and I wore it constantly, pretending
to be him. His instructions were simple

in the extreme: not to care for it,
not to protect it from the elements,

for the way of caution leads to weakness,
and the wearer would ruin the quality of the worn.

Instead, he urged me to carry it in to the shower
in the mornings, and crumple it

strongly in the hand, throwing it across the room
with disdain. It lasted my attempts

to destroy its casual form, its legitimate brim.
When he left he promised he would send me one of my own

in about eight to ten weeks. It never came.
I intend to carry my bare head around in similar fashion.

The Lament of Thomas Stearns

I caught a fly this morning
taking its constitutional
across my bare wrist, domed
it under a teacup.
The perfect china shook.
I went upstairs to shave.
The razor held a special status
in my thoughts, bare bodkin
in the bath water. Downstairs
again exactly an hour later
by the cuckoo clock, still
a wild penitent insisted on outlet.
No air soon would give it notice,
the table setting calmed.

All my life I have wanted
to take my fist down,
right onto glass. Begin
a violent process, send birds
scuttling off the near branch.
That would be an event.
Like all the island curled under ash,
bodies with no motion, burnt dolls
in a crusted house, the lava flat
and sullen now that the fire's done,
cold as a widow's night-cap.
Instead, I created a second life
for the creature, tilted an inch
of rim to aperture flight.

The Landlord Hate

I would re-zone the lines
and turn your house
out-of-doors,
and without land,
would let you in,
to my room,

where I'd set a fire
like a well-laid table,
all the bone
china, crystal and silver of it
clean for the meat, the wine,
and sit you down,

and bid you eat
the hearth:
the cinders, the flame, the heat,
the wood,
until your stomach sweltered
and you died.

But before you did
I would call
a doctor
who would put out your food,
and you would rest,
and burnt, be returned

to your senses,
and love me
like we had never met.
This is the dream
of the absentee lover,
the Landlord Hate.

Gun Crazy

Against the world, just us.
Behind, a trail of gas stations,
small banks, the meat packing plant,
knocked over. FBI Telexes
clatter like town gossips across America:
*Barton Tare and Laurie Starr, dangerous
and armed.* How did it begin?
Neon wakes me, I peel back blinds
to jackhammer rain, shake a Lucky
from the pack, and light.
Behind, on the tangled bed, you are mine,
every inch of your easy hunger, your fear
cold and material in the night.

Where are we two going? When we get
there, how will we know we've finally
arrived? Mexico, possibly, but the bills
are marked and the Feds hot on our tails.
The first time we met, I shot six matches
off the crown on your head, at a carnival,
won five hundred bucks. The moment
the matches flared, I knew my bullets
would always be true, direct. You kill
out of a necessity verging on need, I
cannot squint the eye down to that degree,
my hand trembles at the sight of flesh targets.
Still, I'll end up putting a bullet in your heart
up in the Lorenzo mountains, in the mist.

That first night I aimed and squeezed
I should not have missed.
You wake and call me over to the bed.
Then I'm down in your arms and kissed.
Your mouth sets off all four alarms.

How can a man be so made
from moments of early loss?
I was always gun crazy,
so good at one clear thing:
hitting what I could barely see.
I see nothing in the darkness now, only
one part moving on the bed, my body
pressed like a pistol
into the small of your cries.

Evening on Putney Avenue

When all the lawns are shutting off,
neighbours each with a porch light to close,
I stand in my driveway and smoke alone,

not allowed to smoke inside my house,
and look down Putney Avenue, left and right,
as I was taught to do before crossing,

but stay in my place, watching for the moon
to change, as people wait for green.
A boy and girl shoot past in a red car,

she turns her face, an instantaneous affair,
then it takes Mortlake. A family with another
girl slowly talks through the leaves,

acknowledging no part of me. I step back
into the lilacs, to let them go without
having to recognise my slight presence.

She also turns, her eyes see my new haircut,
but she goes on with her parents,
her skinny legs in black summer shorts.

She accompanies my mind to the end of the block.
Once, this was the street where
I played soccer-baseball, and kick-the-can.

I must know the ground here like no one else,
the way the caterpillars crawl along the arm.
I lost a lot here, and when I was gone.

I toss the cigarette off the curb and prepare
to go back in. My parents are in there, warm.
The spring air is chillier than you might expect.

For all the things I do not have, I have
this night, suburban and sublunar, to collect,
like a paperboy cast in stone.

Mary Veronica Swift, 1914–1991

1.
The cosmology of a room is uneven.
It has containment and leakage the heavens
cannot hold or set, it has been lived through,
beds the weight and blood of persons
having moved, and traced, their outlines
by breath and dying. Mary Veronica Swift,
you fell in passing from your comforter,
your head abruptly struck
where the white radiator's iron coiled.

2.
I have brought away trinkets from where you died,
Christs bent into each conceivable trident of pain,
and will fit them to purposes on my Verdun wall.
Paint leaps at the hammer, cracked like ice
in the Arctic as it heaves, to both sides, broken.
Plaster flours my fingers, leavened hands
setting aside Mother and Child
to inspect the damage:
a Nile zigzags from baseboard to ceiling.

3.
Now I hang your Dublin cross,
made of fine linen,
saved behind glass in a frame
no bigger than a face;
suffer no debt or anger
but the loss of love.
Wielding a substance known as light,
I rise to strike, like Hephaestus
tempering his blow
against the pagan nail.

Ways of Counting

When next I see you see me,
You will be young, I will be thirty.

Years are like fans in plays by Oscar Wilde.
Ladies open them, part of the scenery.

In your hands shake out our days.
They beat the air, cool our faces.

Each fold, tinted variously, is a time,
And the beauty of the whole was planned.

Now I am alone, until rejoined,
When you decide to finish the book of us

Borrowed by a friend. It is body
And mind, mind and body, being so extended.

When next I feel you feel mine,
I will be like a fork given back its favourite tine.

Kanada Post

I remember some other life as if it's mine.
My country has become a stamp, weather,
and what my mother says, over the phone.
I miss less than expected. My small house,
the brick dust, the white slanting porch,
and the things we don't mention anymore.
Soon front yards were new others, mowing.
Schools that'd been one way, were not, now.
And the snow. It falls and builds great towers,
closing off what is within from what's without.
Snow-blowers with their dark, regurgitated slush.
Trees catch ice, become impressive with April.
My birth month is rain and light, a dancing pair
of skaters. The smell of winter breaking like glass.
I never loved the ones that deserted, and not those
that did the replacing. Neither were mine to lose.
It's not a country if it only happens when it's gone.

Letting Go

It is the simplest thing
to open up the fingers,
let the teacup
tell its fortune on the floor.

Or in the movie, drop
the villain, from a President
down Mount Rushmore,
to squash him flat.

I've been one to do that:
leave the kettle on, the bath
running, the baby in the stove,
jump off to be in love.

Hull Losses

First, the Concorde's tire burst, then
the *Kursk* went down in the Barents Sea,
all hands knocking out Morse
with spoons on bent hulls, the high-tech

surroundings inexplicably silent.
Rescue pods fail. Scan-addicts,
meanwhile, search for HQ babes,
dragging up thumbs from blue depths.

Cold Russian submariners morose
on an Arctic floor; exploded German
tourists in the burst supersonic;
a child penetrated, later dumped in a bag;

the convict injected; the neurological patient
whose eyelid, alone, is what still moves
(fluttering like the flap of a cut thumb).
Each a real presence: but not for all time.

What is our true quality, sly impermanence?
The flaw in us may be like a single hair
scanned in by accident – a stray line
fracturing the collector's perfect jpeg.

Intergalactic Travel

Anyone who has travelled late
from their lover's arms (for water
from the milk-white bathroom,

half-asleep and dreaming moons,
like a voyager to the stars, who
doesn't age while all the world

rushes through time's paces)
then returns to sleep's different
partner, as if an aeon had intervened

(the way she lies, her odd breathing,
shape thrown askew in new geometry,
now almost alien in the half-light

refracted through a sparkling tumbler,
how pillows have been re-ordered
as if a strange enemy regime

had seized power in the absence)
must keep faith with all that was and
not lose hope, or think the sense

of things had been tipped totally,
as if shot through galactic optical glass
or some sort of moth-gnaw in the fabric

of darkly-tailored space – should know
they will not be forever lost
in these odd-angled spaces

of distance, a double bed's mangled
topography, but recall that keepsake legs,
the intimate tangle, will once more become

the familiar sought-for homebody
when rejoined, the warm mothership
of sleep muffling us all to singularity.

THE CHILD, THE FAMILY, AND THE OUTSIDE WORLD

Glass and rubber intervene.
You pull sheathed, inserted arms
from the container where she stays,
then look back, touch unable.

Leaving is like carrying fear to term.
Mother, the click of your heels
going down the polished hall
is just her heart, your heart.

TRICK

Karla is eight.

Her whole body is folded like a napkin used in a trick.

Folded and folded over again.

A red napkin.

Folded and folded, then swallowed.

Out it comes, from somebody's ear.

Slowly, knotted.

Nobody says: it isn't the same one.

For her next trick Karla will stay under water, silent.

Until she wants to.

In My Father's Briefcase

Pink and blue file folders, as if his work
Divided into boys and girls, circa 1960,
Stacked, beside uncapped black markers,
Whose ink was gone. Acceptance letters,
Which he'd sign at the kitchen table after
A careful review – in his tense scrawl.
Maybe, also, green gum with chlorophyll
And an old *Montreal Star* sports section.
If I had asked, and he had remembered,
There might be a few *Richie Rich* comics.
Twelve pennies orphaned in the corners
Would rattle when he closed it up again,
Then put on his difficult suit with her help
To go to where he was never fulfilled.

Hume Knoll

The trees on Hume Knoll have grown
since the highway cut down ones
they replaced, a hundred yards on,
no longer smaller than any of us.

When workers come to widen the route
they won't know they're walking where
Melita and her husband Ian took care
to block diesel-torn wind with firs.

None of the woodcutters will recall
that fifty years ago this was a bare hill –
snow-rounded – crossed with daffodils –
now another year raised in ice –

but as stiff green guards fall around
the cutters will recover older ground –
finding, during work's pause, grass
my grandparents mowed – as it was.

Last Year's Model

What happened on the forest floor
is old, forgotten, a short story.
Moss covers her mouth, many months

branch over soft rot, stale metamorphosis.
Very few identifying marks remain
with the rain and feeders having come in,

a face masked with bark and mushroom.
The breastbones picked clean, steam
is evident from humus and flesh

in the ageing litter of darkness around
the scuttling beetles in the abandoned park.
No one addresses this unfashionable

woman, worn to the bone, sporting
a lipstick of soil, eyeshadow of root,
her chin beneath a toadstool's pout.

The New Fedora

In Budapest gentlemen wear fedoras.
I do too, mine soft and black,
made from rabbit's fur.

Today, it nearly crossed the ring-road
sans my head, lured by the wind.
I grasped the brim

and held on with my gloved hand.
I smiled, catching my father,
being him. All the long work

of figuring manhood out, responsible
and dark, suddenly lifting
like a shy clerk just given a raise.

Water, Running

Our marriage is water running
in a bathtub with no plug.

For a moment, I want to disagree,
then don't, impressed by the image:

your image, for what is, after all
only you and me. Or, me and not

enough of you. But then, language
doesn't always connect so truly

to somewhere else: fall over and across
another thing just so, neatly joining

worlds together, like difficult puzzles
working out suddenly, from new-angled

words and other meanings piling on –
like those many-layered fountains

you loved, at the gardens in Istanbul,
which in their motion are symbols of

an Islamic paradise in letterless
signs more pure than if written;

like cold champagne cascading
over wide glasses at a wedding.

Seven Eights Are Fifty-six

Sometimes I think I would like to be
a bold children's character who
can bounce into other worlds, through
mirrors, windows, closets, doors even,
and end up somewhere else, terrifyingly
alone and having to rely on creatures
one normally refers to as scary,
in order to defeat the source of evil,

and return, wiser but not much older.
I wouldn't choose to travel by any of
the kid's preferred routes, myself.
There's a certain bright gateway
I've had in mind to journey by, for
some time, one of those picture-boards
they have in grade school, a poster
but not quite, which the teacher points

to, to teach you things like how to tie
a shoelace, or tell time, or count produce.
This one board hails from the Second
World War, and it has a mother and her
daughter on it, and they are both dressed
to the nines in their best canary-yellow,
and the lady wears one of those hats
familiar to any fan of Mary Astor,

and the calendar says April 8, 1942.
They're in a grocer's. The woman's finger
points at some slices of ham she'd
like to have the butcher wrap up, so
she can take it home to make butterless
sandwiches, and during this procedure,
the little girl, who has long socks on,
is squinting at a cat, sitting on the counter,

gazing into a *verboten* bowl of milk
(as you do) and reflecting deeply on
whether to lick deep and sink ships,
or do its patriotic duty, and leave the dairy
stuff to children who need their supply,
or maybe this is only my gloss on the scene,
but what I want to do is leap into the frame
in my best yellow suit, and make the bell

ring as I enter the shop, then tear the page
off the calendar, letting all of time's hell
rattle loose – while the butcher and the wife
embrace, behind the large simple blocks
of colour, the little girl picks her nose,
or begins to skip rope, or leaps into a puddle
(mud would be good for all these people) –
and knock the milk back, leaving the tabby

amazed and jealous of my human ability
to see a situation and grab it by the tail;
or maybe I would simply step up beside
the couple, missing their dad, somewhere
in the Pacific, or maybe flying for the RAF,
tip my Panama hat, and order some baloney
so that I could sit outside in the wartime sun,
eat my way into history, or out of its cartoon.

After Hardy

I thought of Thomas Hardy –
how he missed his wife,
wrote about the places they

had been together – went
back to, after she had died.
It must have been difficult

for him to return then (*there!*)
to those spaces. To feel time
again, when it had mattered

and she was real, not simply
like a hand's condensation
on a window of your train

which passes all familiar stops
to halt – finally – at a station
where no one you know lives.

The Last Days Of St Lambert

First, the houses went, their white paint
curling up over in the flames
like sheets of paper thrown from a window
caught in a wind. Nothing could be saved

but the porches, which all withstood
the blaze, as if wood from another tree,
this one of stone, had been substituted
invisibly, one morning before the children

were born, when sleeping was longer.
Then, all the churches disappeared,
as if nothing had ever been on the lots,
the ground fallow, the soil black and good

and with a small collection: one girl
an arrowhead, a boy, a pierced American
coin, through which his eye could see
a roaring sun, and her red hair.

THE MORE DESERVED

We know nothing better than what
we never get to call our own, space
it should be filling, its masterful lack.
We marry our unachievements, make

resentment a second home: a garden
we keep out back, for little pleasures.
Her ring slipped off a finger, the line
slack now at the bottom of the ravine,

promotions passing overhead like jets:
the day we least deserve grand failure,
we will receive it at the door, delivered
by gloved hand, tipping for the letter.

Penthouse Revisited

What is it I really want from them: caught
licking a fine, full-globed, demi-tanned tit,
interested cupping an umber, saliva-tipped

nipple in a red-nailed clutch, curled fingers,
their lace skirts hiked up to spider-silk taut
inner thighs, sun-browned or goat's cream

pale, to reveal a trimmed, diamond-shaped
slit, pearled with audacity, their stockings
charcoal grey, or scarlet, pushed half-way up,

in smeared light Master Vermeer himself
would've wept to apply – with such intensity,
as the strokes imbue Vaseline with properties

that almost earn claims of artistic integrity?
Why do I wish to move in tonight, just so,
to their plentiful houses finely decorated

in French Provincial, or American Gothic,
as if a connoisseur-slattern subscribed
to *Better Homes and Gardens*, had stocked

a whole house full of boudoirs filled with
copious feather-spilling bolsters for lesbian
sleep-overs, and four-poster beds for Sun

King-sized brief encounters, and wrought
iron bedsteads for kerchiefs to playfully tie
slim, girlish wrists to – but not too tightly?

Why do I respond stiffly, as if to patriotic
hymns, when I alight upon such pictorials:
she's toting black sunglasses, nothing else,

her cocoa-buttered, navel-ringed torso laid
over a simply blazing turquoise backdrop
of parrot-green palm and chlorinated blue,

or in the hot horse-dusky barn, on hay bales,
she fingers her bumhole, beneath a frilly
violet bonnet, legs swinging loose in a yellow

summer dress, sweet under a Georgia willow,
fresh from a debutante's ball, or slave auction?
Is it only that, in seeing all of them still there,

in their never-changing, ever-available poses:
arched, semi-reclined, or dangling upside-down,
after so many decades away from when these

women were my yearned-for implausible lovers
(no more likely than Hitch's heroine, Novak)
stuck under my bed, pressed like meaningful

leaves or petals in a book, but here between
mattress and cold box springs – I am nostalgic,
brought back, like at Tintern Abbey, to earlier

awkward vertigos, on puberty's bridge of sighs –
and find myself, oddly renewed here at this web
site, after all my actual partners' genuine touch,

human insight – left to pause, praise and collect
these thumbnail scans of mere images of Eros –
adore their flat, impervious, imperishable teases

that were promises of the little that is so much?

Visiting Westmount

A live-in maid admits us this evening.
Conscious of my station, I brush off
all the snow gathered at my ankles.

In the hall what look like cello cases
turn out to be rifles, packed and ready.
Prints of pheasant-shooting parties adorn

oak panels. We go into the library for tea.
Her father, recently deceased, can be seen
as an obituary, framed and mounted,

almost another trophy. I take a green
leather chair, fascinated by her Germanic
cheekbones, and her Evelyn Waugh air;

she's faux-aristocratic, not even anglophone,
a family dislocated by some blitzkrieg
or another, but, half a century onward,

comfortably settled in a mansion built
for whiskered bankers from Edinburgh,
whose fortunes, if laid from Atlantic

to Pacific, would make quite a railway
(and did). Those men created heaven
on an old volcano, the Golden Square Mile,

wore watches on long chains, never smiled,
and prayed in Presbyterian cold spells
that hung around men's souls like squalls,

but drove their blue-nosed schooners
far, will-power and predestination fuel
that can turn a rapscallion into a plutocrat.

I'm charmed, to be sure, and honoured
to be such an invited guest, having won
her attention at a debate between Selwyn

House and my public school, at hers, on
The Boulevard, in front of several hundred
girls in plaid skirts and knee-high socks.

She says, in an accent lifted from Oxford,
your eloquence very much knocked mine off –
which does wonders for my self-esteem.

She pulls *The Wealth of Nations* from a shelf,
shows it to me. Inside, preserved like a rose,
is a photo of her father, inspecting a factory

where he designed and manufactured arms.
He's sharp, has modern lines, and lapels
that say his wardrobe was frozen in '63.

I want to marry the heiress then and there,
join this distinguished line of entrepreneurs –
damn the thwarted lineage, foreign pedigree:

so long as they're not French, they're fine.
I turn to kiss her, seal a contract or two.
Her mother enters, ravishing in a black gown,

to announce she exited the opera during
a deathbed scene, so fresh her bereavement;
but, unable to be poised with cups, saucers,

leaves us to the good silver, the tragic china.
I shrink from plans of attaining capital,
and her ballerina's throat. Sophisticated,

she offers to call a taxi. I agree, but prefer
her Mercedes she handles with gloves,
where I could've shifted as she pulled up

outside my own, small, suburban home,
and put my teeth against her pale earlobe;
and in dark's promise helped her disrobe.

The Seven Wonders of The World

The world's seven wonders are elsewhere.
But there are many more that go uncounted.
She was one, he another. We each have
our own list: scents, pleasant performances,

evenings, particular rains, the bright stacking
of fruit in a bowl, a pencil's shading, her
surprising ability to reintroduce a sense
into a forgotten place. The centuries

will have much else to say, to add. I
cannot astonish anyone who has not been
here themselves – within the pyramid,
the hanging gardens, under the stars, flowers

of balanced stonework and light – seeing
portioned marble, feeling curved bodies,
handling a sin; cradling a son or daughter.
The layers of descent through time's sensations

are appalling to enumerate, all the wonderful
things, apart from the dreadful, we may
have, or chance to behold, to obtain
through any of the senses that remain prepared:

her hands with their slender fingers, her diamond's
very, very small inclusions choreographing light,
and the parrots and the monsoons, and almonds
and tanning butter spread across bronzed skin,

and the salt of the water, and the fright of ice
cut into clarity under the loupe of the moon;
not ever ideal, for too real, but for all that,
worthy of any ancient worship you might devise –

or for that matter, a leopard's eyes, a violet swan.
We could go on and on, and yet we won't.
How to bother with sensuous excess, when it is
all around, and always present, like omniscience

is said to be, except this concerns pleasure,
the fulfilling absolutes that exceed our potential,
as if we had cupped our hands under a waterfall
having expected the barest minimum of a dribble,

and been inundated with a torrential satisfaction.
How can we desire when we are sensual Pharaohs
with all the gems and servants of the senses
spread before our wonder, as if arisen in a tomb,

our cats and many mistresses and rubies spilling
from out of their comfortable waiting stations?
To say there are seven wonders is to undercount
shamelessly, as if we told the hours by one hand.

Rue du Regard

Ask the blue for more darkness,
it may oblige.
Then, winter is a sky,
night the way a boy
touches her tongue with a finger,
not finding it cold.
Beginning this is lack's reverse.

The Golden Age of Travel

The train station is back there.
Farther on into the quiet
Town, tree-lined avenues
Guide like manicured fingers
To the heart of blindness.

That would be the square
With its unorthodox churches,
Town Hall, and Museum
Of Photography. Every colour
Has moved here, like war-torn

Refugees poured into a camp.
Here they flood up the walls.
Orange, purple, wild greens,
Yellow and several shades of red
Up and down the walls.

But it is the absence of anyone
Who speaks a native tongue
That leads to blindness. Only
The sun presents itself as universal.
No one will so much as serve

An ice cream without elaborate
Signs and gestures. Sadness
Invaded this world once.
The men, dressed like circus
Attendants, move as if their bones

Had been broken in a net-less fall.
They spit gobs the colour of the walls.
It'd be nice to become a local citizen.
To learn to spit and mimic like them.
Learn their sad religion. To marry

Here, and send five children to
The purple school. To visit the
Photographs in the old museum.
It would be central to one's vocation
To assume a new identity here

At once, unfold a beige suit,
Take off Shipton & Heneage shoes
And wait for the sun to set behind
The aquamarine church
With the spires that might not be

Christian. To go through life
With Penelope, one's lawfully
Wedded wife, to see five children
Off to the wars and festivals,
To bury the family, and widowed,

Spit against a grey-green wall
Mind emblazoned with inspiration:
This was where all art was,
All passion, and all dust, all
Through the long slow century.

By the Pool

"We cannot keep, and see." – Anne Ridler

We sit by the pool, its ideal rectangle hyper-serene
at the stone farmhouse's edge, on a ridge which,
isolated, *Straw Dogs* style, looks over
fields of unready corn, burnt-black sunflowers.
The shocking, inert spread-eagle of a lizard
lies still at the bottom, unlike its earlier
fluid manifestation, tongue-like,
or built of fire, so ruinously out of its dry court.
I dive for the submerged king, rise with him
clasped like an encrusted sceptre, stiffened –
throw him out onto the sun-throned rocks –
once his casual rapid domain – piercing
his reptilian splay – he has lost all dignity
on some stick or other, jutting up, as a hawk
poses over the scene, and in the nearby paddock
lambs combine to replay a common
anxiety. We turn to tanning, read day-old news.

A day ago, at approximately three
o'clock, as we began to turn from white
to the palest of reds – a weak burn –
the inappropriate telephone had begun uphill,
ringing with the mystery and full weight
of church-bells, or the entirely-too-loud
grandfather clock, built in Claric, which
each night had knocked us on the ears, each
hour, not once, but twice, pure and cruel –
so too, the phone. You ran up
into the shade, over white pebbles that hurt
your bare feet, forcing you to skip, childlike,
leaving a French *Vogue* and the *Sunday
Times* to flick back and forth, ignorantly, in
the wind, as if being read by invisible hands.

A minute later, you were released from all
the boring pleasantries and mediocre rewards
a heat-seeking pool-side holiday portends, its
facile kingdom of vodka and burnt steaks, snacks
and chlorine — the bad tans that carelessly fade.
Enda – sweet, tall, lovely – had died.
Unsure of which realm we inhabited, grief's
or escape's, we tried badminton, between essays
on the existence of heaven and perhaps not.
The worst, to contemplate; and too commonplace for
words. Stranded on sun-red tiles, we exiled
ourselves to the palace of shuttered dusk,
but, the next morning, entered a church, again,
and proceeded in blackness up the aisle,
enthralled by the cold airless must of unused space.
Newly-burnt visitants, in the dog days of summer;
our intercessions lit by a salamander stain on glass.

On His Wedding

Rising early as if for a duel, seconded
By a best man, I wake to sky that's *bleu céleste*,
Rented tails, and fresh anxiety, but bride
And groom do not turn backs to pace. We
Collide at an altar, as though it was a super-
Conductor. As old Wagner marches
You up the aisle, my awe wells up at what is
Brought in: veiled, molecular, still flowing out.
Your entrance is an atomic favour, for witnesses
Observe us, met here not to cut, but sew space
Rent in multi-fabrics. Our cells push and pull,
Mysterious as that new-smashed meson X(3872).
Side-by-side, apart, like shadow and
Direct flame crossing to overlap, as a rosy flower
Sometimes is mistaken for its name.

Cinéma du Look

Looking isn't love,
but it also pays attention.
The deliberate openness
with which blinds are left
apart, curtains wide, lights on
at all hours of the day and night.
And I, who must
work for a living, bear witness
to her changes, the shifts in
scenery, the *Cinémathèque
française* of her bedroom.

Homage to Charlotte Rampling

Not to be just a "skinny sado-masochist"
twisted past all recognition, suspenders
over fishbone torso and tweenie nipples
singing in the death camp to your lover:

that was, Charlotte, a wise career move.
So was the departure to alter ego Paris.
Marriage suited you better than nakedness
set in the most perverse circumstances

imaginable. Older, in *Under the Sand*,
Ozon's film, your eyes identify the body
of your drowned husband, no longer human
but swollen by the sea, putrid and sexless.

Your gaze lies over the available absence
we all tend to as volatile organic creatures.
The loss and horror and the contamination
under the white dry sheets in the mortuary,

pulled aside like the skin from a surgical
wound. Your eyes hover, they stay open.
We see you struggle, there, in that moment with
what we all have to face. Your face dies for us.

Marylebone

So, I had a fight with the Frenchman
Who smashed our crystal wedding present
Against the side of his moving van.
He'd taken exception to the small size
Of the English windows, narrow stairs.

We'd debated the merits of his abandoning
Eighty-six boxes of personal belongings
To the British weather, much in evidence.
He looked the sort to snap near children,
Then write memoirs in Genet's old prison.

His shaved head raised the hairs on mine
For how he'd self-barbered it, done free,
Discounting the odd supergrass *cicatrice*.
The landlord's henchman, his Union
Jack hung up next door for all to see

(With the Internet surveillance camera
Connection) lounged in a biker jacket
That Gunn might've taken out on loan
From Brando, and quipped *that action
Was like pissing over yer young bride.*

Cross-channel tensions weren't eased
By this observation: urbane as Niven.
Saw him and his cronies off with London
Pride in a pub at our corner. Walked on
And came across a plaque marking
The name of A. J. Ayer; who'd died there.

Be It Resolved That

In my first novel let me be a boy debater,
A thirteen-year-old in a grey suit,
Roget's in my smart black valise.
How I admire the smooth prime ministers,

Their lips, which I should like to kiss.
Be It Resolved That Desire In Puberty Is
A Bicycle With Training Wheels.
Should we repatriate the constitution?

Death Penalty: pro or con? In green
Cafeterias, over Sloppy Joes, on plastic
Trays, we manoeuvred, as best we could,
Tight in uniforms, assured of our power.

The judges watched us match wits,
Flushed under the flourescence.
How they rustled uneasily as we came
To adulthood over question time, at

Chest-high podiums, that girl fainting,
Some guy diving for the wastebasket
To upchuck. *Shit out of luck*, we'd say,
Before sneaking a fag with our partner.

Leader of the Opposition, that was when
I first met *you*, all dressed in green wool.
Love's a dizzying school in one lust-rush.
How many in Brazil, how few in Japan?

The soft drink parties, after, were in high
Homes on long hills, and someone got
To go upstairs with the one they had beaten,
Earlier, in Room 302. Never me.

I was unresolved. You said: *take up*
Kick-boxing, but I was rather shy for that.
The rhetoric of sex: thus is regret defined.
You learn to love Cicero, aim for politics.

The Tenant of Wildfell Hall

I miss being a kid, but barely recall those parts
About chores, not getting kissed, or being ugly.
And the palpability of novels. Opening
Helen's copy she lent that Sunday afternoon,
By Monday I was hooked, on gothic winds
And girls in cloaks, and love, for characters
That were actually her, or so I felt. Returning
The loan, she looked at me, as if I was already
Forgotten, but didn't bother to ask me not to stay.
Death's not about going to the block for a woman
Whose better husband you robustly replace.
Living is more like falling forward on your face,
Onto a scuffed parquet floor, lightly dusted
With all those who have been swept off it before.

On the Back of the Book

Whittaker Chambers channels Wilt Chamberlain.
Edward Said channels the Marquis de Sade.
Saidye Bronfman channels Charles Bronson.
Pierce Brosnan channels Walter Pater.
Nick Hornby shakes hands with Richard Nixon.
Dick Van Dyke shakes hands with Dietrich Bonhoeffer.
Bono shakes hands with Benjamin Disraeli.
Gilbert & Sullivan shake hands with Lou Dobbs.
Dorothy L. Sayers meets Salman Rushdie.
Anthony Powell meets Powers Boothe.
Jim Boothroyd meets James T. Kirk.
Henry Kissinger meets King Vidor.
King Kong meets Vidal Sassoon.
Siegfried Sassoon meets Siegfried & Roy.
Roman Polanski crossed with Paul Theroux.
Theodore Dreiser crossed with Teddy Kennedy.
Ken Dryden crossed with Alexander Pope.
Carol Pope crossed with Bob Hope.
Walter Benjamin crossed with Bing Crosby.
Nevil Shute crossed with Edward Norton.
A mix of Agatha Christie and Kris Kristofferson.
A mix of Edward Nangle and Nancy Reagan.
A mix of Elvis Costello and Marcel Proust.
A little bit Chandler, a little bit Chomsky.
A little bit Yeats, a little bit Yasser Arafat.
Two parts Churchill, one part Capote.
Two parts Pound, one part Presley.
Two parts Bradbury, one part Basil Rathbone.
Move over Adlai Stevenson and Brendan Behan.
Move over Otto Preminger and Atatürk.
In the same league as Hitchcock, Hammsen, Hammond.
In the same league as Porter, Pinsky, Patchen.
In the same league as Auden, Austen, Auster.
In the same league as Bellow, Bukowski, Buster Keaton.

The Influence of Anxiety at the Seaside with Tea

She saw the beauty of the sea and could not rival it
For lack of depth, for cut and clarity. It screened
Itself like a blue movie. It was a mandolin. Flat,
And on a continuous feed. The sea was a pool

On a spool, a fluid, wet circuitry, a freakish
Cola, without sugar or fizz. The sea was in business
To sell waves to sand; to deliver cetaceans to nets;
The sea is a grey-green, moon-led elephant

Who always forgets. She sank into the Sargasso
Of herself, and touched a wreck. It yielded doubloons
And Maltese falcons and other encrusted valuables;
She scooped the ice-cream starfish and the jelly

Of the sperm whales, and the cardboard villainy
Of certain sharks. She slid like a shadow, a dagger
Of slim ease in a pressurised medium. She sang
Oxygen and filtered sunlight, and salty tunes.

She was overcome by *Harmonium*; flush poems
With *quince* and tea and royal-rococo references
To the world and imagination; dove, in homage;
She wrapped herself in a peacock-daubed kimono

In silken envy. How could she not be immensely
Injured by the creations of Florida and San Juan?
The ocean and its sisters set out its store of baubles,
And she bought them. She was the eye and womb

Of the stanzas that melted and ran through the town
Like rough blue-white bulls storming a seawall.
This was the first performance of the storm, the horn
Section was off. The rain pulled toads from its hat.

Ballad of the Solitary Diner

When I eat alone, I am alone.
Thank God I have my books.
Friends? Not many.
My wife, in her tower, earning money.
A few who live in other countries

Too far to go to share a meal.
When I sit down at noon I often feel
As sad as a man having married
The moon. You cannot love well
Someone you can't share a spoon

With, be it soup or salad.
The waiter or waitress assumes
The identity of a temporary friend,
But they are busy with their errands
And soon go to other people.

Then, as my tea cools, and the day
Gets weak in the head and fails
To keep appearances up,
I put on my winter coat to pay,
Leave a pound for their trouble,

And go out the way I came in.
Thank God I have my books.
I can tell by the limited smiles
As I turn, I no longer have my looks.
It is a shame we have to eat at all,

It hurts us to have to be so open
And quiet, even as we appear social.
If I could get by on my poetry
I'd eat a page a day in my flat.
I'd stay thin, and not become fat

As all this dining out in the world
Has made me: yes, and with nothing
To show for the tedious work
Of getting it down, but one more check
And a dark walk home, through a town.

O Magnum Mysterium

How still they sit, to listen to the air become music;
Britten's austere carols to *Wolcum Yule*!
Stiff-necked pensioners crouch forward in low pews,
Anglican or just off-the-street. The choirmaster knows
His Dove from his Davies, Poston from Cornysh,
In Dulci Jubilo returns us to when December
Promised God's giving, winter night
And the star, at last, to deliver us from evil.
How venal, then, to notice all the time-worn suits,
The dresses past their fashion. Decrepitude cradles us.
It was ancient men who surrounded the babe
As he emerged, peering from sand-blind eyes
To stare at holiness. As if it might cure

Their own worried flesh. St. Giles saw dark Cromwell
Married, grand Milton buried under the floor.
There's no rose as virtuous or fair as Christ but when he rises
Will those who came before do so as well?
If not this may be the last world in which I share a carol
With so many bleary souls, sighing and coughing
At the wine-fed interval. Is it worth such pain,
This short intermission of great upward sound,
To break the loam to creep and bow among dusk again?
Perhaps we should thank Christ there is no return.
We go from wholesome aficionados of Anon to a thing awful;
With all its brains, pluck and rhythm turned and wormed
Like some discarded instrument devoid of all five strings.

Anton Bruckner Choir, A Ceremony of Carols
St Giles Cripplegate, 18 December 2003

Tomsk

"…the Siberian Athens, known for its lacy wooden buildings, furs, gold, and universities." – Local Tourist Guide

What are lacy buildings? Was there ever
a cold Socrates, a Parthenon gilded in ice?
What long poetry, what Pythagorean tears
scattered in these bitter white winds?
What polar bears bit at what rinds?
Did Plato and Aristotle, pulled by a team
of snow-caped malamutes, decamp in Tomsk
to envision gold-smeared Greece
reborn in a frozen swamp, newly lit
by Diogenes' lamp? Did they flame
the chill-gnawed Siberian landscape
with images of icons and geometry?

What exists love says should be:
a dolphin-grey, a book-kissed, city.

Gentlemen of Nerve

I have become my neighbour or the author or the man
I saw in the photo, when I was thirteen; I've slipped in
To his life, the one where you get to be the has-been

Movie writer; get to be the fellow who adores his wife;
The forty-year-old who walks slowly down boulevards
In springtime, thinking of nothing much, sidling along

With a mumble, instead of a song, in his punctured heart;
Now I know what they were doing when they were
Doing it; not exactly, for that was their lot, then; but well

Enough to hum the approximate ontology they unknit.
I have slipped in to the opening along their side,
Entered the weave of their nearby manhood, to coincide

With the shyness of a gentle soul who holds out
For some other day, some boon, a grand foretold
Coming in to confidence (and confidences); a Chump

At Oxford in a silk-lined coat who'd jump a fence
To avoid a bullying leaf or an unkind glance; a gentleman
Gentled by nothing so much as having sort of grown old

Without having ever advanced, in terms of career,
In terms of science, beyond the fields of expectant fear
That the sweet girl who holds him tight might evaporate

And all his books, thoughts and friends will disappear
Like stars, which look quite risky in the sky. So if
I am this guy, where is he now, past having had his own

Slippage moment, when he came into his three-piece Geist?
He might have driven far, stopped at the coast, for a well-
Earned cigar, maestro of leaning knowingly into a sea breeze;

For, the exact moment I turned forty and had insight into *him*
He was set free, to flow or saunter at unidentified ease, no
Longer a person observed or wondered at, but a ghostly skim

Of atoms, then other particles wafting to some inexact home,
As a genie exceeds the prison house of his wishes, to fly late
But gladly beyond the bottle's stoppered rim; so now I hesitate,

Poised, a diver on the doorframe of my impressionable bungalow,
My blissful villa, my flat, my porch, my mansion, my estate –
Until some kid spies me out as curious, unimaginably aged, so

When their grey stubble hits the marker they'll zap to my face,
Slip in to my statehood, reassemble a mixed-blessings-self or two,
While, sweet as rain after drought, I dance out and over as I go.

Emperor

after Solntse, *directed by Aleksandr Sokurov*

I.

I, Hirohito, among strewn boxes
and a fractured aquarium, compose
a poem based on a cherry blossom

and a dissected crab's revealed softness
as purebred goldfish on the lab's floor
strain for filtered water, 'Sea in a Glass'.

The Imperial lab floods with sunlight,
burning the eyes of rare porcupine fish
pried from their reefs for my further study.

Is it snow, or hot ash, progressing calmly
outside my blinded window, placing fire
on the flayed skin of this season's face?

I was a God in fancy human dress,
selected a fine top hat from London.
Forgetting my station, not minding where

I step, or what is stepped on beneath me
(a white, scuttling spider crab maybe) –
MacArthur floating on Tokyo Bay

I removed my divinity like a glove;
petals away from a Chrysanthemum Throne.
The cold instruments of surrender signed –

a document to be skinned of whatever
fabric mere holiness is made up from,
I now stand before my smallest mirror

to observe ordinary nakedness.
Here is my entirely mortal hand
that may close upon a sea urchin's spines

to suffer the same pins and needles as
any human in the land. No longer
will trembling men button up linen shirts

or kneel in my bunker to explain how
a superior force borrowed the sun,
laying waste to our ancient paper towns.

2.

Today feels as much like winter as when
my father, Emperor before me, seeing
Northern Lights, impossible above Tokyo,

summoned me through four ministers
to speak of the sky's bright coruscations.
I have had to endure the long time

in which my wife and children lived
as if I were destroyed, under bombardment –
knowing their mourning as my own.

I missed the appointed afternoons,
when advisors would escort them to me,
so that I might present them long letters,

or read aloud from a masterful composition;
amateur of all, polyglot, ichthyologist,
I know the hours divided against us alleviate

our souls, make us speak new ways.
The sea forever inspires meditation
in peacemaker and noble warrior alike.

I measured my divinity in ocean-study,
so as to know, like common people who adore
the great ruler floating far above them,

each pulsing complexity under
the surface of alarmed, tentative waves
that always tremble like an organism

shocked or rattled by a sudden change.
I have looked at photographs of film stars also,
and felt great sadness for all living things

that move, to experience the minutiae of the day,
in a rock pool, which a greater eye envisions.
This much I learned from marine biology:

each way we mourn or find a motion
is determined by a higher instrumentality;
as if all creatures were forever in a bomber's sights.

Our bodies are examined by light's callipers, then
let drop, as if caught for momentary pleasure,
into the sea, which abandons, recalls, lifts and is.

I'm in Love with a German Film Star

Somewhere in Kansas or wherever Wichita is,
I stop to dally with a waitress in a summer dress

under a diner's neon kiss; I wear a UPS
uniform, drive for them. The name tag lies

when it says: G. W. Pabst. I make a highway
angel by slyly helicoptering sleeved arms

on the line that divides the independent cinema
of this scene. I have the ball cap and the smirk,

am filled with an unbearable urge to be always
thirty-two and to marry a girl named Miss Miss.

I'm filled with the luminous possibilities
of American landscape as it unfolds in movies.

If I was a plane I'd never have to land –
I'd be the land, you see, I'd already be the land

and the way wings spread over and below,
the way a shirt is also a stain is also a shadow.

Modest Proposal

Every word counts, he said.
    And then he counted them.
        I saw my mother's dress.

It was in a garden and she brought
    Out a tossed salad, laid
        The plate on my lap as I read

William Carlos Williams;
    May; my body sixteen.
        How old was she? Thirty-seven

Or thereabouts. The tomatoes
    Were lovingly sliced.
        His look returned me to this.

If it is poetry, no need to ask,
    He added. Use your fingers
        As when you comb your hair

Before going in to see the one
    You will ask to marry, mirrored
        In the hall, the clock a heart

And the words throat-clotted,
    The tie poorly handled. There.
        How many words for the task?

Not the number, the distance.
    The sum of how to rightly say
        Hope under pressure's light.

It isn't what you write down
    That carries the full weight;
        It's what they heard, and why.

And so I went in and was shy
    And turned my phrases. She
        Told me to go to blazes.

I turned, when she held on and on.
    The altar vow has only so many words
        For how darkness binds, goes bright.

Mix Tapes

There are whole mountain ranges,
highways in Croatia,
long broad sweeps of coast and sea,
that were listened through, years ago,

on mixed tapes that now lie boxed;
we listened, as the sun went by
and through and across
and into, your blonde hair,

both of us absorbed, it seemed
by the day and its travels.
Music's kiss lied.
It promised good eternal things,

not just experiences
that felt eternal as they passed;
now, sorting these tapes
marked religiously in green ink

I can recall none of the old songs,
though you still play:
beautifully, in that red top,
above the motor's fray.

Woman at a Station

I see you off, as a woman at a station
her soldier, to the wars, unafraid of battalions
that smoke and whistle from windows as she

holds and holds, before releasing all his body,
his skin, scent, flesh, defined in the uniform;
the train goes, bearing away the adorations of

what was their joined ecstasy, unmarried love,
its little strategies of gin, fags, lamp-lit roses,
hugs and laughter in the park, the rained on rows

to which one returns, not alone with memory;
how the damp bed bears the impress of longing,
how long fingers know the mysteries of absence,

how the body lingers upon its own part in this.
To be a monk is not more or less than such as her;
the cramped travails are the same, the slow dust

gathering a dress of daily orders, flinging it on
one's shoulders in a sort of gay ritual, renouncing
hurt, or what hurt forgets to be, in all the flirting

and folly of the painted evenings, full of colour
and sad substance, the little that represents the all;
his lips and his heat are never against her, but on

her side; she reads the printed bulletins, knows
each manoeuvre as if the application of mascara
on to her own face; sees him fighting in a mirror;

is present in her mind on the field of confusion,
the battle is carried in her carriage, her motion.
So it is I see you off (my god) but cannot abandon

(even as I seek the immaterial spaces without sin
or longing) desire for you, for your attacked,
attacking body. How I aim to forget the cross

in favour of bled-out meditation, fragrant loss.
I hope you shall not return to take me up again
in your pinned arms, whirling me on a platform.

The Expedition

On the third day out we realised
we'd left half the supplies back at base.
The ice held our mood in check.
The radio transmitter was glazed
like a pea in aspic,
could no longer ping
our Morse or morose
SOS past the outer rim of things.

Day six the dogs died; Cedric "neglected"
to put out feed for them.
We ate the huskies, threw their bones aside.
Day seven polar bears, attracted by the remains,
began to stalk us. Day eight: *Cedric mauled.*
The rest of the camp sat appalled, gnawing
maps, the catgut from snowshoes.
Day nine, blizzards and no water.

On day ten, we reached the snow-blind pole.
Leopold, fingers half-blue,
showed me the rimed photo
of his wife and daughters. Day thirteen:
tent blown off by gale force winds.
Day fifteen: *Leopold dead.*
Sixteenth day. There's me, myself and I:
the rest not quite so fortunate.

My Universities

Debating the relative merits of Orchestral Manoeuvres In The Dark,
Or Tears For Fears, while April ice melts slowly in Westmount Park
Now appears to be less world-shaking than when, Misha G., we both
Could be smartly vehement about Richard Rorty, Boy George, Truth,
Logic & being spanked by Marianopolis twins known to us as Ruth.
Not that we were L. Cohen's heirs, but rather a pair of young pioneers
Gazing into the Future with our smoking jackets for uniforms, sayers
Of sooth but more often faux-decadent imbibers of lascivious perfumes,
Who often drank tea (before it was Pennyroyal) on mornings as Winter
Dripped away as surely as Youth does – as children crushed on looms;
If such industrial imagery seems a tad stark, consider the Reagan Years
Were also ours in Montreal; we danced: slim Japanese New Wavers,
The Cure & The Smiths, if not allies, our aural neighbours; felt Time's
Axis turn as early Eloquence (our praxis) dried up in Age's Summer.

Natural Curve

I watched a tree all day, it did not move.
This suggests to me a kind of love.
Nature is what you say it is.
Say it is Heaven or Hell.
What you choose.
In this dwell.
God proves.
See her.
Go to.
Ah.
O.

Communal Garden

May takes hold of summer's handlebars and wobbles on.

The Last Blizzard

My mother showed me
the house she'd lived in
fifty years ago

when she was a girl
who threw glass
at her enemies

with a pig named Margaret.
My father kept his eyes
on the deteriorating conditions

ahead, saying: *soon we won't see
a thing in front of us.*
For now, we could.

The town my mother
no longer lived in
had big wood homes

with long, wide porches.
Fir trees stood nearby.
Christmas lights. At the end

of her street the river was met
by a green bridge.
As we crossed we saw icy water.

My mother pointed out
a view that had once been
on our two-dollar bill, before

counterfeiters forced them
to use a more intricate design.
She showed me her school,

where she had walked and run,
then where she moved to later on.
So what if the weather made us slow?

We stopped to watch
a white deer standing
in a white field, not moving.

Winter Work in April

I become winter and winter's man
to serve winter in its slow work;
my beard grows like the long span
of some white bird's wing. A stork
is a bird, just as winter is a season.

Having put on winter and winter's cloak
I stalk the white halls, a full blazon
of snow aloft in my long hand
like a new torch. I fold out to expand,
as winter's clock ticks on and on.

Riverside Drive

Take that good road, driver
along the St Lawrence
river. Spring sails ice
as boats sail now.

Take your time,
I want to see the houses
built centuries ago,
by the Seigneurs.

Turn here.
We're almost home.
I can smell winter.
I see the old porch ahead.

This is the avenue where
I loved and read.
Thank you for coming this
way, my favourite

route – a little longer,
but I enjoy the view
across the water,
the skyline. Where
do I live?
This address, in my head.

The Wedding Photographer

It is a private, lonely thing
To do, gathering new pictures
Of delight. I take photographs

That build their album, the looking
Backwards, developing beauty:
Their standing, happy, just married

After the light has altered them.
No one sees me on my own bed
Later, rehearsing a vision

In which a white dress lifts then falls
With the sequencing of seasons,
Just and ordered in what happens

To bodies that love, are desired,
As fire, that takes a forest down
As dogs will a stag, cannot know

The king inlaid, uncovering
Vows future-arrowed, as cut skin
Shows the purple all wear within.

I Empty My Wallet

Movie we saw (*Frida*); lottery ticket that didn't win
(01 02 06 09 30 31) bought a week after we married.
Receipt for a coffee shop in Hungary I used to name
Café Alibi. "Your final fitting is" – a stub for my
Wedding suit. I'll keep that. From Istanbul, costing
4.000.000 TL. With the blue mosque on it, number
648817: is it whimsical to wonder who was 648819?
You were 648818, of course. Le Nemrod, our place
In Paris. Lundi 15 Septembre we paid 37,70, total.

I see 1 CRÈME BRULEE; 1 ASS FROMAGES;
1 FILET DE HADDOCK; 1 SAUC ROTTE
TRUFFADE. Was there wine that evening?
One forgets one's own habits, such clutter
Redeems the time's trivial paraphernalia, partially.
What else? Now what started as a chore, a duty,
Almost becomes an excavation: but I won't go
So far as to claim it forms the basis of an art.
It's still work though, to go through the forms,

The tattered bits of paper, one thinks to tuck away,
As if to be reclaimed, a proxy for a moment
That seems propitious enough to deserve a memory,
But too brief or petty to be guaranteed one, untokened.
ENTRÉE A GRANDS APPARTEMENTS
GALERIES DES GLACES. Yes, I recall a quarrel
Here, amidst much glass and circumstance.
SALLE 1 GAUMONT MONTPARNASSE.
A film but this time no title. We saw it 22/11/02.

A counterfoil for Twenty Pounds, stamped
111 BAKER ST LONDON W1 17. FE 04.
All these dates, and no exams to test them.
Here's one for shoes. A CARTE DE FIDELITE.

We won't be using this again. Nine squares
Will stay unstamped with the blue smudge.
We weren't faithful, in our fashion, to these people.
I go deeper, looking for something with resonance.
Your dentist: Nadia. No. The ticket to Bath,

From where I returned, after the crash. No.
Then this: a scrap, a note that looks full of ideas:
*Colin Wilson?; Ben Hecht?; Doc Strange?;
Bermuda Triangle*; and the number, *52*.
Is this the core of the novel I never wrote?
Some fascination with a chain of personages,
Places, that came to promise good creation?
Finally, a small silver thing from Knock: PRAY
FOR US. Someone should, at every little station.

The Mountain Lion

i.m. Ian Hume

We thought of winter
    when we saw the lion.
        Down from the mountains,
  no prey,
he made the impossible sudden

in snowfall.
    As close as, say,
        that tree.
    Still, very much a part
of each instant going.

While defining speed
    for us, our hearts, slowing,
        became the ice
    we'd raced on.
Such is vision's mystery.

It puts beauty deep
    into winter's chill.
        Fast as breath saying itself,
    he was gone:
a lithe accident,

meaty flood, rusted-gold;
    a fur-wreathed kingdom
        on the rangy slope;
    a mouth of stars
at earth-level.

The Recording Artist

"*Wonderful, wonderful* " – Johnny Mathis

My father, among other things, was sometimes sad
And he also sang, just like Johnny Mathis, to us
At night, seated on the left hand of our pillowed heads

His face turned slightly upwards, gracefully, to the side:
The image and sound of him I had when he died –
So that, despite the many hours when he cried out

This memory, not the others, will rise to mind –
Not in order to prove that love is better than suffering
But to record, in my deepest groove, his tenor's loveliness.

Action Comics

Tom Swift sold *Action Comics*
Outside the Amazing Gladstone's
Theatrical Acts of Illusion

To men and women in Forties hats
Who'd pay a nickel for diversion,
Some men stooping for *Blackhawk*,

Women reaching for *Plastic Man*.
Far beyond the magician's curtains,
A fighter pilot was sawn in half

By a German's ack-ack, or some Jap
With a sneer would make the heroine
Disappear with rope and a blackjack.

All this action without applause,
In the theatre of war, that long winter
Sometime just after '44,

When my mother was born, in Quebec,
Unaware my father would sneak
Up on ice skates and blind her eyes

With mittens like the fold
Gladstone tied round his assistant's
Pretty face, but not as cold.

The Man Who Killed Houdini

My father, when alive,
Loved to suck his stomach
In, and urge us
To ball a fist and strike
A blow, straight
To his solar plexus

Erect as Houdini should've
Been, but in the story
Never was. I'd put
My small hand softly
Against his strong flat
Gut, and push, afraid

To lay him low,
To kill him like the great
Houdini – so well did he
Describe the murder-jab
To me. And he'd fall down
Then rise in laughter.

Writing

Say what you will,
it can only tell
what you know.
The words, in order,
have to confess
how you starve
or bless
the beautiful.
The caution or
progress
must reveal
which parts
you'll trust,
which discard.

Envoi

Send out the loveless children,
those faceless ones, pansies,
droops, suckers and ragamuffin
losers, tooth-short, bedraggled,

gaggle geeks, off-strumpets
and low-levels, send them out!
Let them prowl devil-streets, selling
pock-skin, pencil shavings, eye-

lashes and TB-dolls. Fix them;
spike their drip-feed with Benzedrine.
Keep the comfort-zones clean.
Send these poppets, these tinsel-

Hansels and sappy-sonnets, these
Gretel-stanzas fetching nopes, into
the hands of craving-warts, stucco
borders, palsy-gangs and semi-dopes.

The nasty-edit dopamine cabal are
zoot-impaired, pleasure-pained, unused
to pretty things, flowers, a kind note.
Send my soul to the print-alley fiends.

Hydra

I did not know my own good breathing yet,
Waited on the land while you swam out far.
Rhythm cuts to feel the Hydra teething.
A heart's withholding ache is a line fear.
Voice trips the force after the stutter but
I halt to extend, to give, to utter
As a lover on the brink of water
Ponders the leaping pool where sunlight lies.
Sun's all surface where rocks break beneath
And many are the divers who have died
Joining their form with the forms below,
Hot to imply their safety was fluid –
Their falling lines a force to fly and flow.
Ceasing to be I sense my mind in blood.

The Mosquito and the Map

You dawdle on the cartography of conquest
In the tent where Caesar stabs his ring finger
On the Tiber. Dare you nibble the Emperor
As he repels a disappointing triumvirate?

Or have you already tried it, pre-emptively?
Is that why the God-King bleeds tidily,
Nit-picks his neck, looks wan at the future?
No. Daredevil blood-pilot now you dive.

The Shape of Things to Come

appears to be a trump of doom;
is like a hollow room; a horn
of plenty; a ballerina's

shoe; a house in Whoville,
a devil's mouse; a bang-drum,
a pirate drunk on deadman's rum;

like a broken broom used to brush
the webs from day-dreaming boys
in math exams; a rack of lamb;

a doughnut convention; a depleted
pension; the sort of position
churchmen don't like to mention;

is shaped like a poem mute and dumb;
like a big bronze bell held by
a handlebar-moustachioed

strongman working for Barnum;
like a sausage and French mustard;
seems to be hoist with its own petard.

The Ministry of Emergency Situations

During an emergency, all
Wedding rings must be removed
And citizens will be asked to
Undress in the streets. The Ministry
Will bathe those affected with
Disinfectant Foam. They must ensure
Their eyes are shut. Those who refuse
To take off jewellery, tokens
Of affection, clothes, will be shot.

The fully naked will dance in
The medical shower, then be
X-rayed and scanned by magnets.
Inspections will go on. The cleansed
Will be allowed to request
Compensation for their torn rags,
Irradiated keepsakes.
The Ministry of Songs will form
A choir, and douse them in anthems.

The Oil and Gas University

The sectors interface. In Novosibirsk
She wears a hooded parka. She
Challenges outmoded ideas. She
Transforms the education-research

Manifold and provides new incentives.
She pulls her hood back to reveal
That beauty achieves real excellence
In a real-world setting. Her lips

Hit each of the seven key targets
Set by the national institute last year.
Ownership and exploitation
Have no place in this exciting dynamic.

Opportunity, however, is vital here
In this oil and gas region near the pole.
She walks past the infrastructure.
The gas flares in the fields, the tundra

Reciprocates under the white solar
Glare – then continuous darkness
Of course will eventually supplant this
Brilliant feat. High technology

Must provide a nexus and intensive
Inventories. She is beautiful and I
Wish to introduce myself to her
At the Oil and Gas University.

Winter Winter Tennis

When a child, I was a reed.
People bend. Straw burns, too.
And burning mends. The air has faith
in smoke signals, having had them
in its ways. Sheaves are fruitful.

The person you're kindest to
is the one you want to save. Fire owns
the ruins it creates. Ash on the brow
means only one love inside the mind.
Thieves in the temples means a cold.

Want to grow old and take down
this book. Want you to know me
as someone who once had a look
and a place to call their town. Voted
for a mayor who kissed a rose.

There was also a pink child in the frame
and what's her name. He won, he won,
they over-proclaimed. Ran races
of boys through villages, trailing flames.
Am this, this way, this very same.

Wouldn't see it any other way.
Should this enter woodlands where
poplars recreate, overturn the maypoles,
suckle ancestral possibilities ho! of tone;
born alone hey! in a cloud of verbal turns.

Taking Tea with Charles Bernstein

Lapsang Souchong with a lapsed sous chef;
Charles enjoys its smoky aroma and tarry taste.
Keemun with a Communard;
Charles delights in a lightly-scented nutty flavour.
Yunnan with a U-turning UN man;
Charles likes the maltiness with milk.
Gunpowder with Guy Fawkes;
Charles notes the soft honey taste, the little bang of it.
Chun Mee with Connie Chung;
Charles raises his eyebrows at its smoothness.
Oolong with Long John Silver;
Charles eschews milk and sugar, not wanting them to dominate.
Ti Kwan Yin with a typist quite intuitive;
Charles swoons at the fragrant infusion.
Pouchong with Pol Pot;
Charles is suspicious of the very sweet, stylish taste.
Pai Mu Tan Imperial with a pretty tanned empress;
Charles notes the small buds of this rare, white tea.
Yin Zhen with L. Cohen;
Charles spits out the silvery needles.
Jasmine with a *Jass* band;
Charles sits in with Bix and finds delicate modern time.
Rose Congou with a Belgian from the Congo;
Charles admires the great skill used in the handling of the leaves.
Earl Grey with Duke Ellington;
Charles considers this mandarin blend a tad traditional.
Darjeeling with Jar Jar Binks;
Charles celebrates with the "Champagne of Teas".
Dimbula with Dmitri Shostakovich;
Charles sips the light, bright, crisp tea; his mouth feels fresh.
English Breakfast with Edie Sedgwick;
Charles likes this strong bed tea.
Afternoon Tea with Anthony Blunt;
Charles bites into a cucumber sandwich.

House Blend with Olivia Hussey;
Charles is comforted by the type most people use at home.
Bubble Tea with Bazooka Joe;
Charles is amused by this beverage with tapioca balls.
Iced Tea with Richard Blechynden;
Charles, hot by now, is refreshed by this ice cold drink.

THE RED BATHING CAP

Red bathing cap
At the edge
Of the lake.
All of her prepares
For the water
At five o'clock,
Sun reduced,
Most bathers gone.

Mother, you stood
So before me
As I read, when
You were young,
Without the long line
Of the operation
Divisive on your hip.
You swam out

Clean and strong,
For an hour, then,
Until your head was small
On the surface,
Or not visible at all,
As I would, from time
To time, look up
From *Mimesis*

Or some anthology
To make sure you hadn't
Drowned. Beautiful, tall,
You'd go directly in,
Continue, as the lake's
Black surface dulled
At evening, and flies

Prepared themselves
For the bats to come;
Your arms bringing you
Through reflections of
White-barked trees, stone,
So far, until you'd return
Shivering, to shore,
And I'd race to bring
Your towel down,

As my father built a fire.
Enwrapped, you'd stand
By it, and dry your hair.
Now, there is no fire
Here at this public place,
And Tom is dead a year.
You're older – water
Cannot keep us young

Forever – and limp
To where you start to enter.
I want to go with you tonight,
Keep pace, but you always
Swam out alone, serene.
Red cap – (brightened like
A pricked thumb) – how it goes
In and out of the going black

Steady as your pulse, a sewing
Needle, threading water
With your breathing stroke –
Is like a light, a light to me
That says the where and why
Of home, of coming home.
I'll bring your blue towel as
You stand out in summer dusk.

"There is, in it"

There is, in it, something of the autumn,
Something of a lake bottom; a favour being
Returned, unopened. A letter burnt.
A lesson unlearned. A muffled oar, risking
Silence for lifting through water. Numb
Fingers reconnecting knots. Women laying out
Fuel for themselves in a damp, starlit lot.
But what is mostly in it is what is not.

Stars as they turn into their unbright coldness,
Daughters as they slide still onto the ground;
Each unborn animal, each unstruck match,
Each ambush left before the riders enter
The narrow pass. The snake that forgot
To spend its tension spilling in tall grass.
Windows no stone decided needed breaking.

The high bedroom emptied of mourners, the king
Lifted out, recovered, only to slip and fall
Next morning, and so resume a smallness
On his own. The cold floors of parliaments
After the last to cross has gone and locked a door.

The pocket watch she found, and wound
So that it said it was eleven all day round.
Its chain was golden, and it contrived a line
Across the rich lawn, gathering dew,
So that, on being brushed aside, it was rain.
A brain pivots on what is beyond it
Like lies hide around the corner from coming true.

Seaway

Perennial ice plagues the ships

The child is not a child but a receiver

Observe how ice is like a streetlamp

Lit in the blue night of winter, electricity

Only one form of many in which to reach far

The ships as they seek the Seaway are ice-rimed

The black tracery of the Locks opens

Receiving their lit silent transit, laden

The children sing sea-chants

Of ice-lit nights, sailing further out

Beyond the ocean, ocean, then Japan

Trees

Trees that have been there, always –
like music that cannot go away –
in any park or street of the mind,
each appearing as a dream does,
with laws only it need not obey –
going, returning with the casual powers
of wind, rain – the trees that were there,
pressing on window, on eye, in winter,
in broad day, the time walking home
or running late. How sky moved
ceremoniously in their highness,
how one fallen was a loss and omen
on a path. Will branches shade me then? –
good company in that darkening arbour.

"Ivo," Marianopolis, 1984

Like rain, desiring, the Cocteau Twins
Return, bringing that cold sadness
Again: sweet as a bare shoulder, lost
Pain, an ice flavoured as your skin,
Which was, summertime, the toast
Of my tongue, trying to barely possess
Your black boy-cut bangs as they ran
Like water in mythic April showers –
You and your cherry Docs, alley-dancing,
Your lips as untouched as the Rhodes
I forfeited for high style, laughing gas;
A. Alvarez mourns that no one reads I.A.
Richards anymore, but I do, and we did –
Shivering, music like kisses: recollection.

Spider-Man 2

Sitting in a cinema with Sara: best date ever.
Doctor Octavius doing his Harold Lloyd act
Over and across the Manhattan clock towers,
MJ and Parker new web-crossed lovers.
She turns to me with a *wow!* like Monroe
Might've given the lens with her mouth.
Truth is, movie-going was made for true love
Delighted. It causes hugs and fear to implode:
That molten ball of fusion Doc Ock invented
In an abandoned warehouse: *all the power
Of the sun in my hands!* Emotion as
Mad culmination. She grips on to me
As tentacled arms slam New York masonry.

Library Going

"Libraries in the UK will be redundant by 2020" – BBC news

I return, even though the due date's faded.
The glue's decayed, lets gape an erotic
Separation between card and page. 2020
Is not so much a time as a place, loaded
With laser-visions of dystopic outrages:
One being the library's gutted, dead as

A church. Pigeons for squatters, mice;
Screens unplugged from their machines
Have taken their flat coma minds away,
Now as functionless as a drinks tray
At an AA meeting; as sad as memorabilia
For a team that never had a victory.

The books themselves assume the position:
They spread out on their desert island
Shelves, the castaway long gone:
To rescue or sun-picked oblivion. Bloated
By rain-damage, yellowed, quiet as kids
Traumatised by the playground into books

And music, they spell out culture's purpose:
U-S-E-L-E-S-S. Queuing where they would
Have stamped my tomes, then run them
Over that queer magnetic beam device
(Sometimes forgotten so all hell's bells
Went off, startling the pensioners, the mad

Homeless and the religious elf, whose home
This was, because theirs was lonely, unheated)
I joke about late charges, and toy with an idea
Of asking the invisible librarian out for tea.
Her reply is vacant and worthless, anyway;
As are all these authors, glossy covers,

And flattering blurbs: *best, better*, and so on.
What did those reviews get them in the end?
A better type of casket? A leggier friend?
Anonymous? Take your pick. Even famous
Writers get lost in indifference, once dust:
Their agents have moved to digital recreation.

Still, it isn't so bad in this page-littered
Mausoleum, a permanent autumn of loose
Leaves and broken spines: it's just a ward
Where all the injured veterans of some old
Romantic war lie, under their sheets, to fold
Into the future like a memory of wind-turning

Narration: a novel ride, reading, at the sea,
Or, like a faithful canine, that bedside block
That kept you an insomniac; that door-stop
Whose catacombs contained words, characters,
And even a sense of falling into love, or destiny.
No one borrows now. They read, if they do,

Off monocles, implants, it's all direct. No
Going to a building to get a bunch of stories
To carry home, like groceries: all delivered
Over optic wire, at the speed of vision.
I leave the copy I neglected for so long
On the returns trolley, then stop in the middle

To snicker, take a bow, cough loudly,
Then finally sneeze. Once, this was *verboten*.
Not anymore. No one to care to shush,
Or put a prudish finger to their thin lips.
Acting out, I yell: *fuck literacy!* An owl
Or an addict mumbles back; my own voice

Echoes off the subjects, from Art to Zoology.
Time to go. On the way out, on forever-loan
One supposes, I acquire a How To guide

To automotive repair, and a battered thriller.
I know how both end, but still desire the act
Of taking my literate communion publicly.

The Talking Cure

You cut your hair very short exactly three hours after
I told you how much I liked your hair long. Bold.
Bad baby. But the pageboy cut works.
Makes you look cuter even. You dance madly

On our Persian carpet reminding me of analysis.
You move like some cute alternative girl in a club
In Montreal I never met but could've. Bad.
You're zany, dancing up a frenzy, your

Feet burning a hole all the way to the Id, Vienna.
In Vienna we argued about buying a book in
Freud's museum-flat. In fact, I wanted to purchase
The entire set on sale. Now, my dream-girl,

My trauma set to music, you work, go, come, set
Down and slide, to Tegan and Sara, which has
Every letter of your name plus T. Uncanny?
If you're going to get off, you might as well

Get off with me. Your hair whips up a blonde storm,
It could be Ancient Egypt here in our private salon,
The only mark on our carpet your sacrificial coquetry,
Your cute long savage gyrating set-to-music body.

French Poem

I pout and slink, pose for *Elle*,
possess the boulevard,
scrumptious in green cashmere.
I'm taller than the Eiffel, go down
like Napoleon brandy.
Spank me please. Zola
would have known how
to show the realism of
how I tease, stretch
and fold out at ease, like
any jejune character in a novel
by Colette. Have I
been pinned down by love?
Not yet, not yet, not yet, no, not yet.

Mainstream Love Hotel

The night we washed up late in South Japan –
our first night after we'd clashed –
we found ourselves finally falling in
to an old smashed-up Love Hotel.
We could picture our small lit-up room
down by the woman who doled out her keys
as if they were dog collars for the unbound.
We edged ever upwards, floor by floor,
not wanting to use the pinball machine, rum,
coin-slot bed, glowing dildo, or karaoke mic,
while a blue fan rattled, rolled like
we were being beaten round inside
some smooth hot-headed drum. Like in a plane
we half-slept, lights red as looped fuck films ran.

New Theology

Here is the god not believed in, and here.
Broken, as rain is set apart, unmade

In the way a bed never slept in is calm
When deep within it is a radiant pain.

A tree the wind caught and murdered,
The sea cast out of its cold home, onto

Colder stone. Everywhere, the god
No one worships remains, split as

A boxer's lip – participating
In a sequence of things, the strain

To assemble meaning, or a world –
Shifts on the tilted deck of desire.

Inch by inch, my god stretches out
In sunlit beams, lithe and implicated,

Clever as a lizard adroit on a white
Afternoon wall, becoming the measure

Of all dreams, all actions. Faith needn't
Be coarse weave to dress a stiff obedience

For life, as if music entered an ear
Alone, left from just one sleeve – reason's

A jumping horse, whose slight rider
Is also lifted over the waterways to soar.

Green Girl in Vermont

That green girl,
Going through the green,
Leaves like seawater,
Water like a tree,
Green as gold,
Green as envy,
Not ten years ago,
Not even three,
Greenest ever seen,
Known for miles around,
That green girl,
Quick as an eye,
Faster than a nail,
Filing the wind,
Cutting windows down,
Open to the weather,
Seen from above,
And on the ground,
More like a person
Than a thing,
More like a song
Than a singing,
Hardly a word spoken
No vessels broken,
No offerings or tokens
Slipped past the toll,
Out on the road,
Green as the knoll,
Grass grown over her
Now, though still
Thinking of the green girl
That none of us
Came to know,
All wanting to say

Stop and say hello,
How her dress was yellow,
And the moon was gold,
And the snow grew
Like hill-flowers to cover
The face of her name
And the name of her lover,
Beside her as she goes
Green girl, endlessly stopping
In our town for a vanilla
Milkshake, we missed
Those days, those clover
Days of summer and sun
And swimming naked,
Going through that surface
To be naked a few feet below
And weeds tangling
At our head and our toes
Green as the girl
We all loved when young.
Green as moss that goes
Like fire over the stones.

Now the rain's my only reader

The rain's the flicker in the theatre
of the screen and the monster
from the black the ether

is coming in on feet no dancer
could escort, courts favours
on the windscreens of the cars

themselves ensnared in dark's
remarking of the meters
parking where rain breaks its fever.

Now the rain is pearls that scatter
in houses where mystery matters;
leaves in ambulances; prances only

if glass breaking can be said
to prance; practices law
in sixteen languages; addresses

the court with silk and glasses;
the rain is a momentary stay
against dry salvages; dull passages;

clears the throat and casts off
lozenges; the rain evicts red leaves;
leaves no trace; advances, retreats;

the rain comes in on elaborate feet;
is indiscriminate yet selective;
evolves an argument I must have

with wood and light; is textured
like the night, a leaf, a blade to cut;
the rain is sharp as a tongue or sliver;

makes the wind pause and then shiver;
knocks at the gate and will deliver;
the rain's a cessation of the peace talks;

this rain is like the day the rain stopped,
only before that moment, just before;
this rain is like the girl in the third row

scared by the monster, the guy in tow;
this rain makes me long to solve crimes
and entertain evening with end-rhymes.

"God has left us like a girl"

after a line from Sidney Keyes

She has gone, out of the house
And down the stairs, her scent
Evident and sweet as lilacs,
Shaping her descent in the air,
Leaving us alone to pray
That tomorrow, again, she will
Deign to, lightly, reappear.

Canadian Fiction

This was the severe part
And the rotunda shone,
Was sea-like in its movements,
So that her sailor beamed,
Was a beam, moving,
And the lighthouse element
Was perfected. Read on,
For story, if not pastoral,
Read on! Christ was
Not beheaded, the dancer
Desired the other torso,
So the first man died,
The proclaimer.
Epic contains cruelty,
Spans water. I grew up
Near a long river
Bringing vessels to grain,
Grain to the sea
And in motion achieved
Commerce; locks
Adjusted levels, men
Moved up and down,
Objects went through
Hours to arrive elsewhere
And children lined
The piers to wave them on;
And the dead are buried
In uncongratulated areas
Nearby, offhand, almost,
Offloaded, ignored
In the merriment of shipping
And bread; in the daylight
Least considered; the living,
Also, are unattended to,

Except at visible intervals,
And during intercourse,
Communion, and feeding times,
For all must acquaint
Themselves with nourishment,
With food for throat, for soul
(the soul is the throat
and we thirst as well as hunger).
Often I regret ill-conceived
Projects, uncarried, still-born,
Never premature, never created,
Unmade novels; stories
Uncharactered – no meat added

To their lineaments, no curve
To their air, their architraves;
This failure is resonant of
Many loves looked away from,
The shipments delayed,
The bored tanned faces
Of the men leaning over
The rims of their boats,
Waving at children
They neither fathered or knew,
In the listless blue air
Of August, en route to Peru.
I knew teachers with moustaches
And white shirts, who slept
On Saturdays, crying
Among the grass and spiders,
Their scalps half-matted,
Whose parched lives
Ached in their village,
For some identity only art
Bestows, only critical writing
On art bestows, when description
Collects loneliness with praise,

Calls them in, and holds
Their abject purposes in stock,
Lines their days, like pockets,
With glowing praise,
With the waving, undulant,
By the vessel, as it rises,
Story by water-story,
Above the locks, into industry,
And summer heavy with cargo.

These Days

These are the days
Not other days
These are the days I was
Working towards
As other farther weeks,
Working for days
That now I see have come in,
Fish from the street

Sold fresh, the man
In his whites, ringing to bring
Fish just off the boats,
Days that were in the sea
Not so long ago
Not brought home to me
I'd thought to have my work
Done by now, to have reached

The goals set out long ago,
I won't ever get there now
Nor need to, here, see
What was earned, not owed,
These days of you and me
More than pensions, savings,
Toil, long hours, ever bring,
Days beginning with us in bed

And ending with us asleep –
Between is the time worked
On, to make, and keep
No other days
No other ways
These are them, here,
In the basket, glinting like coins,
Fish fresh and shining from the sea.

Late History

For too long, she said, you have been looking
out at the countryside, with your eyes so far
into the fields, it could only be the rain which
keeps your body in, or do all the people that

have died ask you to stay this quietly in your
chair? No, he said, no one is there to make
requests in the garden, and the rain wouldn't
deter me, either. I have imagined time to be

sitting here, finally tired of motion, as the sky
becomes darkness. There has been enough
movement beyond the glass. Even now wind
is tempting that tree, the one we climbed, last

week, or when we were children. History
is a single branch of its tall bowed reaching.
Who will speak out for the tired times, who
may gather the cold and sun inside, to allow

no sorrow, enduring a still and silent ecstasy?
I will take the dark garden inside, she said,
but first I will take your hand, and bring you
out into the long grass, where night has been.

The Teetotaller's Song

The woman in Waitrose
Considering lamb, or,
On Marylebone, hurrying
In the cold first hours of February –

Each enticing met face
Reminds, not of pleasure
But of pleasure's final consequence –
An exhaustion, fine and judicious

As strong boys wrestling,
Shirts off, on August grass,
Neither yielding their bit of lawn,
Their held shadows poised,

As if deciding whether to break
Or forever remain intact, enclosed;
So I love the appreciation
Of an arm, a throat, a gloved

Hand, drinking the unreasoned source
Of this adulterous notice,
Alert to what is expected of the world,
England, unbound from January,

The ones on the street I do not stop,
Entice, embrace, and kiss –
Writing this in loving's stead,
Giddy as after being christened,

Lifted up, to the watered day,
My sober, spun, anguished forehead.

Skylon

The sun's been uncovered
by MI5. Teens pass,
debating BBC television.
London in sunlight
is almost human.
Let us build a thin
aluminium column,
revive Labour in our time.

The Quest of the Holy Grail

And I shiver with anticipation
At the coming into me of a swan

Lancelot or Bors at dawn –
Love lets us pivot, turn

A spear above or below will burn
In the same internal intense urn –

A body is just an interpretation
Of any delight in all penetration.

War Poetry

My childhood… well, try *Poetry 1914–1918*;
It wasn't hell – not quite simple or bad enough.
If childhood is a country, I don't want to visit.
Meanwhile, as an adult, I wear suits and ties
And am quasi-okay. I try to keep my head down.
Tickets are now online for being a kid again.
The Troy I had was levelled pretty much by ten.
Sometimes it's their words, sometimes unknown.
It's There that is the problem with Here.
There is where their Fear sets up its beachhead
Turning a sandy honeymoon into D-Day.
How wonderful if we could go summer
In a place shaded from the past, with only
A view of the future, wiped of Then. Just you.

It's not a poem unless it's seen

It's not a machine unless home-grown.
It's not a phone unless it types by horse.
It's not a hearse unless you get out born.
It's not a greenhorn unless it blows.

It's not a rose if it smells like glass.
It's not a pass if you fail to kiss.
It's not a miss if you knock it out.
It's not a parka if it's sprayed on.

It's not a tan if you wash it off.
It's not a cough if you want it to be.
It's not a bee if it floats like a bag.
It's not a nag if there's no dream.

It's not a scream if you smile.
It's not a mile if seven leagues.
It's not cigs if you're running rings.
It's not a song if you speak.

It's not weak if it is song.
It's not wrong if you write it down.
It's not a clown if it won't mime.
It's not rhyme if you can't recall.

It's not small if it fits in your head.
It's not dead if it stands up to pee.
It's not me if you dream it instead.
It's not lead if gold in them hills.

It's not pills if you don't feel better.
It's not a sweater if a garter snake.
It's not cake if no ice cream.
It's not a beam if no deep mote.

It's not a quote without fingers.
It's not singers if they faked.
It's not a lake if no lady.
It's not shady if you start to blister.

It's not sister if no kid.
It's not id if you forget the ego.
It's not meagre if lots of plenty.
It's not mentis without compos.

It's not piss without the taking.
It's not making unless there's breaking.
It's not talking unless you listen.
It's not glisten unless light.

It's not sight unless a Milton.

Glassco in Quebec
(Huysmans in France, Brummell in England)

A pastoral, obscure dandy
Observes the barns decay
As if an ageing roué
With the ladies of his parish.
The wood is blond skin, Sapphic,

The fields of hay grand streets,
The locals in their carts
To market, jaunty toffs
Bowing to all the prettiness
Their rutted courting meets;

The rows of tools, sparkling scythes
Are canes made of the finest stuff;
The farm's sunburnt dust motes
Setting off the nose like good snuff;
The daughters to their waist in grain

Are dancers for a grinning queen
Who demands they begin again.
These provincial details
He disciplined with classical romance,
A young buck from Paris back

From hanging out that took
Half his chest away.
Rich slow sanatoriums
Bought with ancestral bonds, language
Wilder than childhood's golden pear trees

Allowed notebooks to accrue;
A growing account; and a lung's
Complicated tug – coughing up
Green that desire brings.
Style kept him sane.

Style exposed his lack –
His luck to beach south of Montreal
In pairs of three, even so
Acquiring like a servant or opinion
A quaint normalcy that ran

Seasonal as farming, as
Eternally tough, basic.
Released from artifice,
Whipped into being finally natural,
Or, it may be, infamous, a bit rough.

Michael Kohlhaas

after Kleist

First they starved my two black horses;
Then they beat my loyal stable hand
So that now he coughs up blood; he will
Never recover. That would have been enough

To test most good men. My faithful wife
Was struck in the chest on her way
To petition on my behalf. She died
Three days later at my side. That's when

I sold my home, my business, sent the children
Away, over the border, to be safe. I gathered
The few men who could be trusted,
Who knew me, knew I was a just employer.

They too thirsted for vengeance.
We arrived at his castle at night, killed
The first two men we met, quickly.
I whipped a stable boy within an inch

Of his life; we scoured the place. Wives
And children were pitched out of windows
Like so much excrement. Knights bowed
For forgiveness as if I were the Lord.

I was not the Lord of Mercy, this night.
We lopped heads off like children
Taking the flowers from a field. I waded
In blood, a man fording a shallow stream

To cut a journey short. I lost no man
And turned the Junker castle into a waste of stone,
A field that could not be ploughed. Now
His toll gate was just a dead tree cindered.

I taught these bastards what pain
Is, in the language they spoke.
That was only the beginning. Good murder
Is its own calling card. I nailed up warnings –

For the enemy I most wanted had fled
To a nunnery, to hide behind God's skirts.
I would have bloodied that white linen
But when we arrived, a hungry mob of thirteen

Killers with a cause, he was gone ahead,
To Wittenberg. Wittenberg should have prayed
That instead the Black Death had knocked
On their good gates. My men, unknown, blessed

Like cats on silent paws, brought unexpected flames
In the name of Kohlhaas in the night, nineteen
Buildings gone, including a school, two churches.
I nailed up a new warning – give me the bastard.

He'd taken my horses, and my wife. He'd pay.
They did not relent. Second night and more men
Slipped in, fires like sores on a plague victim
Erupted, the whole town danced to the fire,

Trying to find enough water. Look in my eyes
For water. I had wept that ocean dry. Give me
My man. Not so. The third night, the town bells
Rang like every virgin married at once;

Dawn brought groom and bride to their ashen senses;
The timbers and foundations blistered.
What kind of world can men build for each other
If a good man who makes an effort is turned aside

Simply because of nepotism?
High places with no room for honest men encourage
Conversion to a new faith. Mine calls for heresy:
If they won't give me satisfaction, by Christ, I'll nail it out

Skull by skull myself. They sent two armies against me –
But my mob had grown to a hundred like a pestilence.
We took them as they sought to meet, interrupting
Their wedding night by slipping between their own force.

They wept at our love of murder. We knocked them down.
Now that got attention from Martin Luther.
He called me damned, said I should stop. That gave me
Pause. He was a good man, who spoke to our God.

So I dressed in new clothes, under cover of the night
Came to him then, unawares as he scrawled words
Against the Pope, his own war. I begged to confess
And receive the bread and blood of Christ. Luther's

Moral maidenhead resisted my simple thrusts,
I was turned back from that door. He vowed safe passage
If I'd demob. If the army of justice was just dispersed
They would come to control the situation again.

No strongman is more deadly than the disease of an idea
Incubated in the skulls of men, lice in the bed sheets.
Trusting the man, I left, broke the mob, took myself to Dresden
To seek fair repayment in the courts. Half the mob

Like a broken tooth festered in the mouth of the country,
Raped and burnt, a lingering faggot after the fire was out.
They blamed me, and court intrigue and the inherent evil
Of men who love their friends more than the truth,

Sentenced me to die. Not before the black horses, fed
Up to their original rude health, were brought before me.
As I was killed the crowd rushed forward to touch blood.
My sons were knighted and their bloodline runs on.

Fertility

Bolts past, and past, and through names.
History seems young beside its fluent flame –
The rootless flower, the star without a start –
The reason for being early, or late,
The richest date, the opposite of zero,
The cognate's cognate, the king's bee,
The blackness of blackness being reversed,
The hero who sits up and laughs in the hearse;
The only manner in which death is cursed;
The stage on which all monkeys rehearse Lear;
The queer split shiver erupting ingots across
Time so bars of body and knowing solidify
To be born; it is the spliced film of things,
The jumpsuit, the steamboat's toot, the lute
That strings of numbers explode sideways into.
Without this fractious miracle, this intervention
No one, no mind, no skin, no lips, no eye, no one;
How the spill slip causeway goes against caution;
It outdoes eloquence, requires no passion.
Can there be such control in the spasm of the sea,
Such science in the lightning strike that crosses Z
With A, dashing across all letters, chromosome by
Chromosome, unzipping, sped by dot and hyphen,
So real it makes accidents of each, women, men,
Makes love sometimes a field of gold intention,
Waves of tousled, febrile, sweet information?
Its shadow is arctic nullity, the barren place
Where loss is chaste, and memory is not
Chased, across a tundra of insufficiency.
Not to be the fire but the water that shuts off fire;
Each body carrying a coin that turns on life or not;
Parenting or oblivion; to prosper or be forgotten.

When All My Disappointments Came at Once

I greeted them as guests,
brought them in and settled their burdens
with footstools, olives and cool white wine.

This was a delicate stage –
they'd never met in one room before –
had circled warily in the past, strangers

to themselves if not to me (for I
had often expected, if not them,
others with equal claim on my time).

Now, none of my hospitality paid off
for they began to quarrel
over who would take my will to go on

first – each wanted to be the foremost cause
of my early failure to maintain a living.
Frames came off nails; books spilled; lights

fell like building blocks; stains spread.
During their intensity of competition
I took off over the garden wall, refreshed.

Azoospermia

In the late summer I saw my future.
Not gaudy, hardly mine,
Brought to me by a blunt test.
The trees were alert to the wind.

Parents threw their dismal joy
And busy disorder about
The streets. The park strained
At its collar, barked with playing;

The hours in my head abruptly
Stuck. Now I was sterile.
All my weird kids blinked out
UFOS off the radar –

In a moment that stayed around
Like an invasion long planned,
That held its breath, that froze
My bones to my mouth –

I tasted the invisible loss
Of hopes going out. Maudlin,
So private, but pain occurs
Even when the reason's sentimental.

I attempted profound respect
For nature. Nodded sagely
At my secret body's amazing failure.
Considered new identities –

A renewed gender. Freed
From the requirement to breed,
I momentarily thrilled at time,
Now heaped, big, before me –

No Daddy-wasting anymore –
I'd learn Chinese, particle physics –
Hard to be ordinary when rare –
Free from expecting anything –

I gave my wife the gift of nothing –
I planted autumn in our garden –
I put a small stone in the basin –
I placed black glass on our bed –

I laid us down on sand and turned
Away. I walked around, around
The streets here, radiating inexistence –
My name meant never-been – was-not –

I came bringing no warriors in the horse –
All those dumbly-wasted Trojans –
My fate a silly-sounding freak
Of a word – (not even one dead one!) –

Empty as a collection plate before communion.

London, July 2008

Sonnet

No children;
Cold uncoils in the blood;
Science, true, not good
For you. So old,
Suddenly, or so young.
Lyric inside not to be sung.
Plug pulled, screen gone.
Sun out; mind
Bountiful, playing pain.
These are my children
In my head. Unbegotten.
This is to self-forget,
To have the future
Born forgotten.

Slieve Donard

The sea and the hotel
are dull and plentiful
like time in hospital.
Guests from windows
read books on Mahler

then look down on waves
seriously grey, possibly
ruinous or deadly.
White as healed scars,
a sea sub-zero in style.

Long women in furs
stroll glamour along
the beach, thinking
of Charlie Chaplin
who stayed there once

as did Percy French
who preferred Mourne's
mountains slumping
to the water, to London's
gold-flecked streets,

its lips rose-tinted.
The sun, a film actor
in a suite, fails to make
an appearance on the scene.
The hidden horizon

is modern in its abstractions:
fog-within-fog, as light
flattens into a Prussian
afternoon – austere silence
slowly rising to the ledge

lapping hotel, sea, guest and sky
in sadness, a chill that feels
symbolic, that cries out
look on birth and death
as equal ships passing

out past gnashing rocks! –
ships lit to some distant passage
by a faint little lighthouse
a comic smudge of hope
pressed like an insect

into the fat book of night.
Then, the lamps and beams
snap on, casting the place
into immaculate grandeur
on its ambiguous lawn – tight

by wild sea and high summit –
as a bald man gazes in the spa
out on a dark car park
sometimes bothered by a car
and Magda brings tea to a couple

come to the resort to mourn
their inability to conceive
even by acts of love.
Tall curtains are pulled.
The tide turns. The sky thickens.

The Polish Builders in Hammersmith

They arrive at seven,
Leave by evening's eight.
Behind walls that let in all sound, no sight,
They begin, ungodly, to rebuild a state

Of things described by the agent (estate) as *period*
But not, note, *charming*, or *quaint*.
Who knew it made such noise to repaint?
But that's not all they're up to, these Eastern men

Who look like out of pictures
From the time of Chamberlain
When Poland's complaint
Was unattended to, because,

Or so it was claimed then, peace
Was what was needed. Time
Tore down that lie as the false front
It was. Now, hammers in Hammersmith

Ruin the next-door poise. It rains
Plaster, what divided parent from child
Destroyed, as if to unsettle delineations
And taboos. Builders are a riot

Paid for under the table, that stops
To smoke at eleven, and look out
At nothing much, but England, far
From home, a girl, or mother.

No use romanticising manual labour –
That's been done before, by states
Who got their walls knocked through
Without anyone being paid to grunt –

That wasn't work but love in eighty-nine –
But that's easy-Homeric, tangling history
Up with legends of decline or war.
I haven't wondered at their unsaid names –

We stand each on our doorways, anonymous,
Unspeaking the same words of ignorance.
I have no urge to show him the wife-in-wallet
Or explain the reason I'm so often at home –

Employed or freelance we stand alone
Enjoying June tea and this promised sun,
Because inside is darker, dustier and more about
What's been than what's to come.

One thumb's been smashed
And the bandage already blackened.
After they go for good, tools carried off as all they own
I know the silence, more than renovation

That ends affairs. Where else they'll go
Will likewise meet them with habitual muteness;
The English wall, new-coated, of chill smiles
That welcome with a clean lick of politest enmity.

Shop-worn

Age sells to youth
So many things it will come to regret;

But not yet – ah no, not yet.
For now, youth buys and buys,

From old hands, lies made new,
Puts them on and turns

To show its mirror how to learn
How wearing beauty

Lets it be true –
If only for a season.

Hunting Party

A heart is sacred, a wounded hart;
Outrun the symbol in the wood.

Pluck out the arrows. The head
Enters after having been shot through

The air, in order to hunt and halt
The glorious animal that will be eaten;

Flesh parts from pelt; horns rise on walls.
The hall hums with music's knowing.

This is the festival in the glade,
The pump-pump of the love brigade,

That process known as seasonal,
Twirl from rose to worm, grass to spade.

"Somewhere the mimetic is having more fun than I am"

Somewhere the mimetic is having more fun than I am
Doing what is done when description windowdresses
The world in frontage, clear as snowdrops in a cup.
The work of enjoyment is outnumbered by confusion,

Or only the flagrant frost of cans & trousers, poles
For fishing, & other displayed tackle. Brought down,
The claim to see & say; this whirlpool is no hypnotist's plot.
The vision on offer today is grim: brooding germs spoil

In July, but ladder in August to overbreed the solar lung;
Few will survive this transit, so flares beckon the ailing
To camps where sleeves are rolled up, injections slipped.
Now a medical universe is sharp as new-dabbed barns,

Clean as Christmas in white slapdashery. Hung up
By gloomy rafters an unworkable Farmer Brown fishes
For breath, unhooked becomes a clam. No speech acts
As well as a loop for a throat. Tie one on & plunge.

Taking this as morbid helps, as daily assists, as done.
Crisp despair & stylised anxiety won't quite quip a virus
Off the surface. A cut describes its own revulsion in red
Ink, or is a body celebrating when it grins out, festooned?

Race to the poles, where answers are stacked in Quonsets,
Then radar back info-rubber to the chaps at HQ on wires.
Death was harpooned, refuses to blubber any further. Sung
Like that, these undefeated lyrics express strange happiness.

"Down from St John's Wood"

Down from St John's Wood hospital
The sun allows the promenade
I undertake, foiling dark fear
That what resides within my body

Is soon to tear. The leaves are weak,
Unsettle and disappear. The day
Is a Tartuffe of weather: a face
Of gold that may say other things

Elsewhere; the old fact, under a counter
Lies a gun, a bat. The world
Is not just mansions and private security
Though that part is real and looks good;

Inside the perimeters we guard
An unidentifiable aspect like a name;
A pulse or compulsion to think as light;
A presence that flames, gutters, flames;

A soul or mind or intangible perforation.
This beyond-words-shade is all I speak,
Flings me to Maida Vale for a vacation,
A lessening, needed, to coronate

That part alluded to, which, compressed,
Thins out, beaten, to a leaf that breaks;
Snapped in the sway of emotionality,
A wavelike battering of the interior.

September 2009

31 Richford Street, June, after Reading Goodland

The sadness of England.
The coming storm.
The exodus from Tesco.
The death by flu.
The disused factory.
The walk under the rail bridge.
The can of lager in the hand.
The silence of certain streets.
The man smoking by the nursery.
The internet in the video store.
The broken espresso machine.
The 11.30 Mass.
The sunbathers on the Green.
The uneven footing.
The broken pavement.
The methadone clinic.
The shelves outside the shop.
The closed inquiry.
The rain at five to six.
The word path.
The hot and cold.
The end of the class.
The poets of promise.
The ground floor flat.
The geraniums in the box.
The sense of an ending.
The slow growth for another year.
The fear of the impending.
The autumn after the summer.
The unsigned contract.
The request for information.
The loss of nerve.
The godfather agreement.
The leukaemia email.

The post on the floor.
The revolutions elsewhere.
The rubber band left untouched.
The locks on the door.
The friends over after dinner.
The bra being modelled.
The detector vans.
The five novels from Amazon.
The thunder.
The artificial night of a storm.
The brother's child.
The return to either/or.
The despair of small things.

Near St Ives

Upon the sand the lifeguard goes
To lift his flag (yellow and red)
And advance it closer to the dunes,
As a slow rush of tide idealises
The duty, makes its purpose real.

Watching the lone figure walking there
In the noon mist, the windsock's flare
Warning not to float upon the waves,
The loneliness of waiting to be useful saves
Each one of us from our given landscape,

Or the slimmest task. An hour later,
Above Porthkidney on the coastal path
To St Ives, the beige has been submerged;
The clean green water has moved in –
The flags gone and no bathers to protect;

As if crossing the Sahara to me, a mirage,
I hold the image of the red-dressed man,
Stooped under the billowing standard of his select
Role – to be present on an empty beach, lest
Even one soul find difficulty in water;

And such flags as fly to say a person's careful
With another's delight comforts my otherwise
Dubious mind; aftermath of loss
Resolves itself to chores of kindness
Along shores where light settles and enhances.

Hope, Maida Vale

Purcell in the room,
December exterior to glass,
beyond the white radiator's coils
I watch the athletes floodlit
and also enjoy aspects of the park
more wintry and more dark.

Fell into summer gloom
lasted longer, wouldn't pass;
it came to be my work, but toils
of a sad kind; a bad toolkit
knocking at my soul. No spark.
Now vague singing, a bare lark.

Even as you are wrapped for a tomb
hope to see light running out of dark.

December 2009

SLIEVE DONARD II

The suite on the side
facing away from the sea
is the suite with the fireplace
and two plasma-screen TVs.
Better luxury compensates
for lack of view. Before
the perpetual gas fire, stunned
as if into stone, entering

as you enter your Anne Brontë,
a world muted, chemically arranged,
I try renewal of a mind remade.
Mind is book is water is fire, all change.
Fear is the wake-up call at three,
too early for planes. Airport quiet.
Leave the hotel without baggage, fly
direct to Geneva. They await you there.

What occurs is only the turning of a page,
imagined for screen. Unseen is greater.
Is attested to, as we rise in Mass.
Water should be avoided by all those
who get into difficulty with ease, and cats.
Searching for the BlackBerry in the fur-lined
coat, I roam and ring, opening
a closet, from which tumbles a victim,

providing a fitting climax. Mrs. Pontifax
is staying across the hall. The glamour.
She is the Minister of Finance's daughter.
She sees the cold winter sea rise from her vantage.
Our age is blinded by celebrity, seeing
with the gilded orb of a bronze, dull god.
The domes of our room service cool
after we have slaked and fed. As you read

this becomes the first one written under the influence
of an anti-depressed self, whatever that is to be.
What is, is taken off a shelf, a remaining wrack
that half emerges from the brackish ruins of the year.
Will love reunite?
Will Ireland be solvent?
All nights, holiest, least holy,
be still, be silent.

Ireland, Christmas, 2009

Start Again

In a key of slow
Then again stop and go.
Are trees made of pianos
Or the other way?

March plays the bare bones
Like it was evening
In a dive, solo.
Beneath the poverty

A billionaire lies
Domiciled in the soil
And about to pay out glowing
Light and growth.

Recovery is what the ill
Try to do, and succeed
Or die. Health is a portfolio
We all want into.

I am putting these together
Not as if my life depended
On the assembly, that's bomb
Disposal. Or disassembly,

Critical. Wires cross
As leaves revive cool green
And April steps out
Into the sun after a year

On the town, run down, has-been.
Nothing cyclical gets lost:
Time spins and so is redeemed;
Spins because planetary, so

Laws define the poetic sense
That hope is eternal; poetry
Makes lawyers of us all.
I step forward knowing my foot

Slips as part of its patter,
Faster then slower, not always
A goer but ready for a tip or jot.
No longer hot toddy, I warm

To the idea of writing
As a second chance to fail.
The grandeur was always second-hand,
Beauty the accident in what we planned;

The birth of someone else's child
When your hallway has no pram.
Gutted is the direction we head in
Leaving traces of our loss behind –

A fish dragged across the water
On a line you'd miss until blind.
I felt loss when it left me
Saw what I had as it flew

Caught the train by jumping ship
And sailed for home in a caboose
Boxed my eagles with an iron glove
Glued love to my ears, loose but true.

The Safe Years

The safe years are behind us now,
So prepare for what will come to us
She said, and the wind
Blew sage brush and ash

Around our table, where
A woman with red lipstick
Served green tea – the room
Moved to another room,

Time became Augustinian,
Difficult, and rough-hewn,
Feeling emotional, as it would –
We have no way to exist after dying –

Fame, or memory are only conceits –
The years advance, and decline as one –
As paddles raised to tell pilots to fly
Then drop down with the same arm –

And Seneca took his own life;
Kings wanted sons; wanted a line –
No lines supply the ones behind enemy
Lines – which is where all bodies are –

Yes, man and woman dining in the café,
You are fighting, not with each other,
Not, as you think, because of infertility,
Those fears and lost things, little dreams,

Fripperies that perform the shape of hoping
(we fumble about with little dreams
of simple things, like baby showers,
graduation gowns; arms flung to say mom,

dad) – you're fighting with the body itself,
With some mechanical decision made, as if
By accident, but rational no doubt,
Something genetic, some blockage, a

Clicking off or on of some chemistry
That means your plane will not land –
It started on a fine day, blown apart –
Your heart like a storm blows up from

A fine day, will go on over the desert,
Until it ceases, and you and your wife
Are buried together, childless, collected:
Calm in love's entire silence, entire end.

I GO OUT IN MY SUIT, TOO WHITE FOR THIS WEATHER

and feel as if I am walking on a cold April evening
when the moon is about, and moving the clouds
as childhood crowds in, brought to me by the air,
May air on this occasion, and so beautiful a colour;
I think of a question of poets, and readers now –
occasioned by this event (so slight, so full) –
are poets to be next-door types or strangers
brimful with what's out of the mind, unreal
or a tipping over of one then the other, sometimes
all of the above; are they (I mean myself here

to be honest) credible witnesses or better for trying
to inflate the picture? One wants zoo animals wild,
one wants the cage to be wide, one wants rain to fall
occasionally, only; one wants to have control of things
that are, being natural, less falcon and more storm –
some force can be tamed and brought lightly to an arm
and other slight motions of the air swarm to harm, bring
lightning that burns the barns and crazes the mares.

Straw singed by such currents may smoulder, ignite
later, as a memory can burn under the hay for years
before setting the street ablaze with recollection
of a Canadian walk on an ice-cold morning alone
when the dawn-blue clarity of the time burned
like breath; a dawn as near to dark as this London dusk;
to place trust in a poem that tells this story (untimely,
barely challenging or unusual) is to draw in to the hearth
and cup a warmth to the face, enjoying what burns kindling;

a mind can build a fire that never grew in a forest or was cut,
sledded down and quartered in a mill, haloed in its own dust;
the green yearning of this thought and then those that follow
has no precedence in any occurrence for another; rings hollow

or rings a dull bell or perhaps, fortunately, peels like Sunday –
depends on what sky one has walked away from home under
on a summer evening when the wind is just rising a bit
and there is a feeling both of June and September's chill
merged around the corner, and recurring, as water in an estuary
may swirl and forge a mesh of temperatures in its white making.

After Riding the Escalator Back

to switch the watch
a Swatch a second time, a third,
each face scratched minutely,

or because the date was stuck
I became a traveller in the mall
forever unhappy with a purchase

but returning always unalone
brought there with my wife
who loves me and worries for

the sorrow that ticks away
inside the case of my self-schism
but that's not all

I go up and offer each broken
or semi-imperfect object to
the kindly merchant of watches

who resembles a small Paul Simon
which is smaller than you might
imagine possible, and while

outside there is London getting
Sunday under a darkening wing
inside it is the timelessness

of some brief caring act,
not entirely due to exchange of
money, and I am in love

and ruined in some parts of inner
workings, a cog that clicks
upon another toothed gear

stymied again, under the magnifying
glass, still unable to be pried free –
sorrow's just an hour by hour

journey, but in between, there are
seconds as good as before, pretty
good intervals to cling to you and me.

St Peter and St Paul

At Mass the man behind me always coughs
So when we say peace and shake
There are germs between us
I rub off when I've left into the sun
Guilty for my suspicion
Why I am always ill is him
I am glad to be here among people
Who believe, or try to
God I haven't seen, local or abroad
After the death of my father
One September
A tree took on the affections
And silently impressed me
With the idea it might contain love
Beyond all measure
This I think of when I pray
Also, it needs to be understood
That most of the things asked for
Don't arrive
Bad post office, faith
Famine
And we eat out of hunger
I screw up my mind and try to recall
All the ones I want to see again or help
The prayers that rise to them are bubbles
Out of the mouth of fish
On the surface of things are barely visible
In childhood we catch kindness like the measles
And for some it stays
A habit that makes us care
Most are harder than that, having grown
Up into the evenly distributed air
I light a blue candle
For the young boy my brother and his wife have
Godson, Alex

He's never seen me, I live
Across the Atlantic in London
Multiple city of murder
And plays about murder
And commerce
These acts I do
In the absence of his knowing
As I do this now in the absence of knowledge
As to who hears, who ever listens
Love gets called for but may not be given
On earth or in heaven
There is always a spare pew
In front of the coughing man.

Christmas Morning

I have gone out in bare hands.
My tricycle is reduced to contours
under the spokes of ice, rusting

by the pile of wood, infiltrated
with the white sacks of unborn
spiders, frozen to nothing.

Sea Level at Midnight

As she sleeps sleep has to
Fold, into the lengths going
As far as she will go, to hold

The stars that leap, slowing.
Her head carries weight, no
Freighter can list its bearing,

Or bar the slightest sea-faring,
In fog that goes down in cold
Sleights of sea-blacks, off-gold

And barren, the slow hands
Of water, touching. She tells
Me all there is of god, not else,

The false flag of shipping
Will signal the nation flown by
Even in storm or perishing,

When men set off the starboard
And go down in the black dawn
When their mothers are dreaming

Of how they'll come rosy, old.
All that's wedded can be sold
Unless you tell the sea-hag nothing

Here can be bartered, sundered,
For what an altar has put together
No mortal or wave can plunder.

I'd love her even if there was no
Love or god or land to come upon;
So whisper me: is there, or have I

To ship out into the bone bliss of
A sea kiss that hinders breathing.
I'm open to the sea and ice-listing.

Presentation

For my opening remarks
Some closing comments
To sum up let's begin
To conclude three points
Off the record, so to speak
Let's have a minute break
Of silence to jaw-jaw
Mulling it over, we'll move on
No progress without pause
May I draw your attention to
What I won't say next
Note the handouts I didn't bring
Listen to those songbirds
That last week we'd like to sing.

Jean Talon, Intendant of New France, to the King (1666)

Majesty, may this arrive, after months of turmoil
Carried by vassals chafed by violence yet calm
As their tilting little world of wood falls to rise
Bearing them like a nation on uneven histories
Of current and wave, spume and leviathan,
Astounded by dolphin and shark, salt-burnt and wise,
And find you smooth, perfumed, without grief
Or indigestion: vigorous among your scented court.

I write as chief Seigneur, your ever-loyal habitant,
Petitioning for a thing smaller than a flea in rice
Or a bead of sweat amid the corn. August is here,
Chill oblivion of unenviable winter barely run off
So now is the time of white-hot riot and gold growth.
Your lands on the South Shore are pitilessly pelted
With sun that might be melted ingots thrown down
As from the walls of a horde-besieged Avignon

Upon my bald and chapped skull, leather-clad, a ball
The indecently feathered savages might kick for fun.
It is hot – this land runs to extremes like a slattern
On Calvados; we cannot control our slap-happy men
Who have no time to sow seeds not of their own making,
Who would rather gallivant in the scrub and hunt beaver.
I have ten thousand acres of rich fertile land by a river
Wilder, wider and more supreme than the Ganges –

And no one to plant a bean or rip a carrot from the soil.
Majesty, with all my sprightly genius to serve and toil
Yet I am incapable as one mere mortal (though blessed)
To do what must be done, and flourish in this upheaval
Of weather, murder, and sadly-ignorant oblivion, Quebec.
Implore is too weak an expression for what follows –
We need farmers, not rat-trappers, rapscallions, thugs,
Bird-stranglers, or jugglers. We need good wives

To come like sweet blessings in this hazardous limbo,
That feels daily as if there were no Christ, no Laws –
To lie with us in the nights, help us recall the words
We once spoke lightly in our cities and towns
In the human climate of our birthplace. Dispatch ships
Immediately, if you will, otherwise, I shall observe
In a year's turn of the wheel a thousand acres
First of helpless snow then meaningless grass.

On the Joys and Sorrows

They say that blessings pour down on your head
when they do. Blessings, I've had a few. I feel
thrilled with being less than dead, which is here-I-am
collaborating with the physical agents on the wild

run of things, slip-sliding away. Days go, sunrise.
This is the document in which I will nailgun your heart
to my heart and together we'll slide like yuppies
all the way into toy town, rioting in joyousness.

This is the loudest testament I can afford to jolt
you with using script. Now twist and shout too –
you're embroiled in my love, as the poem relies
on your recognition. Canonise me, love, glorify

the shiver of decoration overcoming my soul qua soul,
and all the raw feels that decipher themselves as codes.
Break, dash, dot and squall – fling off your nakedness
and dress like a dashing guard in a prison of Godliness,

perhaps a naval officer with a handlebar, a hat.
The university where I work does not value me, boo-hoo,
as much as the rain, the dew, the petals, the lapwings do.
Ecology is a madhouse of intentions exploring itself

forever for no reason but decaying exploits, the planet
is a nut's cage we celebrate at our own peril, best fled.
Fleeing is what I seek, who came to live among yobs
and loons, and the flesh of adorable girls named Eunice,

Theodora and Miss Coq au Vin. I was Jesus back then,
rise as Barabbas, hairy and pledged to guilt as a badge
of stapled disgrace. I grow sex like a prank on my face.
This is a big splash on the poetry scene, it makes a call

for you to confront your imago and go berserk for art,
which is all we have of Arvo Pärt, and of season seven.
So go coastal, boast and strum your mandolins, rejoice!
The corner with the hapless poet is clear, take your place.

Angels and dreamers ignore all that you have done, why
should they appreciate a jotting of their own monologues?
No, you are lustrous ephemera, a hacking cough, phlegm
on the sleeve of a commandant who holds bitter reigns;

judges, critics, deans, inquisitors, and those who run archives
have better lives than do those who bolt past bounds;
merely immortal, you wait, love-delayed, for old fate
to overtake you; the direct train to Waterloo blasting its drive.

Only then, once dead, will you be read – if even then.
Mostly, rise and sing, strip down to your tremulous knees
and knock on the door marked Forget About It.
The sheer delight is to know your detractors also rot

and when they do, they do so without Beauty's tit
suckling them in the tomb. Grass grows across my lips
which makes me spit. I stick my fist out of the loam and shout
to the guy with the shovel to come running like Hercules.

Together, we shall dance upon the opening that was my loss,
the berth that was my death. Stood up again I am not lonely
now. I have in tow an ill-bred witness to how nothing ends
that begins in verse and hurtles out on its own ceaseless lust.

April Snow

I have seen Christ in April, or so to speak,
snow has come down, unseasonably.
Unreasonably, also. The fragrance on her wrist.

It is possible to make pronouncements about
the world, and salvation, and keep a straight face,
but you may grimace also. You may flap your arms.

Truth is always under reconsideration, has
a revolving door policy. I like the Truth because
it holds a number of possibilities, like a phone.

You may dial Jesus. You may dial eternal damnation.
Feel free to make of your Self as you will. Others do.
Did you really think I would embrace your nation

without complex feelings? Emotion will out,
as parasols on a sunny day. A radiance floods
the world, even when it is least bright.

This is the radiance called praying for light.
The prayer makes the God come into the picture;
words make the God step out of the wall.

This is the exact opposite to expelling a demon.
You send devils running from pigs with a shake
of the fist, with chicken bones and some hair dye.

You use ritual and a winking eye and language
to make words do things with superstition
they might not want to. You possess words

to repossess the pigs that were taken over by devils.
Anyway, salvation is the other way around.
No spitting or writing on the leathery ground.

Unbind your wrists and ankles, here.
You call God on the phone and he comes over
like a pool cleaner, like a call girl.

You pray to God and then there is a God knocking.
And he does not see you when you answer.
There is too much busyness of need in the world

for anything as simple as the visible realm
to be involved in the creation of fulfilment,
all your desires fed at once, the multiple satiation

of snow petals dropping rapidly in April, unseasonably.
Lightness of fragrance. A slap on the wrist, a kiss
and a promise. A door left half open, and a calling,

almost an orchestration, somewhere above
your eye, summoning the weather
to bow to its own conclusions.

Bing Crosby

Heartbreak House was not just a Shaw play,
But a way of life, when I was sixteen. She'd
Play her Bing Crosby LPs and I'd be enthralled,
Cross-legged on the floor, as it rained. It all

Felt very England to me, but was Montreal,
And we were only English by moving in ways
That showed we'd tell a gymkhana if it hit us;
We fed on tea, and Penguin classics stayed

By our beds in threes and fours; I was mad
For her, her brilliant eyes and soap bar skin;
Each posh poised pretension in her sly habits,
Her very vowels, cut through like youth itself,

Which is the only paper knife you will need,
For being young was a fire in me, as you'll recall
It was in you, or is in you, now, if you are young.
I can't sing, anymore, those songs Bing had sung

As she sat so close one bare knee touched another
Until a hush fell that was the absent mother, father,
Making the house very much a menagerie of hope
And what was not lost: never, no, there, virginity.

I had crossed swords with a subtle girl who cared
More for my words than any little body I offered,
Which was paltry; and cowardice hardly endeared
Me, slim in spectacles in nineteen-eighty-three

That summer and autumn when every crisp letter
I received or sent was concerned primarily with her
And the goings on in the ruffled novels we'd swapped.
As love it flopped. As desire it was never improved

Upon, except once or twice, later, when, on beds,
With other would-be heroines, a yawning girl might
Permit me to faintly kiss the fragrance lifting
From off the nape of her thrown back neck;

Half-dozing with indifference in August.
The rest was what I could do by myself, as one does.
No, sixteen and its ardours and ripe slow afternoons
Posing between cautious enthusiasm and rare decay,

As if we had nothing to say that wasn't antebellum,
As if we were gothic in simply inhabiting a crumbling
World of privilege destined lazily to be swept away
As we by ourselves never were at all – all the force

And fuss beyond our walls, trembling like a heat haze
Over a desert only rumoured to exist. Never kissed,
Or only that once, yes, in the snowfall, in the alley.
No, never improved upon, for ache or trembling delay.

For the Boy in the Choir with Tourette's

He slaps his face as others take communion,
A joyful disunion lurking in a devil's abandon
That plays jerky havoc with his composure;
A boy of maybe ten or eleven, corpulent

With brown curls and a wide open stare,
Struck into the choir like a daring nail, who
Takes the music into him and jabs it out
Every third bar by an angelic shout;

I feel comforted he is up there, exposed
For all to ignore or mock. In a sea of doubt
And conceit and sin, his two-faced
Demon that winks about his eyes and mouth

Every so often with a punch to the head
Is all the compulsion I need to recognise
For all the love of Jesus a rich seam of lies
Resides within the idea of heavenly skin

Or a bag of cats roils just beneath us all
And in this sweet off-kilter boy is beautiful:
His stop-go body a rock to save stiller ones,
Says every twitching thing that crawls can sing.

My wife's organ donor card arrives

in the morning's post, so I become jealous
of those that could receive in disaster
her good eyes, take her liver,
give her lungs time to breathe.

I am envious considering my love stretched
open to be emptied, for gross
bodies about to go like night back to day
lively by cold incoming light.

I confess, want to arrest this imagined death
to have those nimble, useful parts
to myself, able to hold on to
a bloody heart, her thinking lobes – still

properly encased in their rightful papoose:
tight skin of the original owner – alive
before shriven of what accidental caritas
so carefully in its loose carcass has given out.

As "Heavenly Bodies" by Tamaryn Played

I came out of myself, was the river in the middle of the old way
of the road, the third movement, a moving van, a targeted thing,

gossamer wing, the last to fire on the smoking man. Go fiddle
with your days if you can, until you break a string. I was giddy,

grown relatively fat, though measureless to myself, on a high
shelf, but toppling; I fell in love most days, gaily, many ways;

floated like heat haze; broke laws like others gauze; runners ran
through the tape of my dreams. Was head of the department of looms;

I ran from hall to hall patterning rooms; was a shoe-gaze instrumental.
They could have put me down as mental if they'd caught me then.

But I was so alone in the music of dreamy unstoppable procession
of being forgotten; a shoe in the back; coin under the shoe; more me

than you, but less of me than no one at all; the sigh before the squall;
breath before the rattle; universal mindless sputtering endless prattle.

The Language of The Fan

Twirled one way, or pushed to the lips,
It means *am engaged* or *a flirt*.
Frail coloured ribbed expanding toys
Feel good in the hand as they grow
Or close across the face, to cool,
Convey, so one's status displays
By the fluttered discipline of a wrist;
Otherwise, a dauphin might stoop to kiss
A lady-in-waiting not a baroness;
Mother-of-pearl; tusk; celluloid:
The sticks upon which paper furls
Are precious, even flammable –
How you tap your cheek spreads disgrace.
The whole fan might go up in one's face –

Disorders of Personality

However it happened it had to
on Candlemas, when candles lit

the glass all down the night avenue
where I for so long dissolving sought

a passport photo sort of identity to becalm
the sense of drift over fist, some alarm;

the booth cracked to take my image in.
Spit out fluency of selfhood, when swallowing

purification of the mother. Christ, a child
bled for ceremony so soon after Christmas.

A wick's spatter approximates bloodletting.
All good is done despite what else we do.

To calorie count the evil, you're over
your daily limit: as each knows truly

in their bed and when passing a hand through
the gap in his chest: the air huffing in over out.

I Think of Delmore Schwartz, Beside My Sleeping Love

Romantic, an American lyric
Pitched to Plato, past a sleeping blonde
By my side (Frisch's *Stiller* slipped

From her hand like a hypodermic) –
As birdsong types out a serious letter
Calling out for madness and History
To meet underground, spring's

Union in the grave, that breaks
When love's excess proves rhetoric
Can be poetry before it persuades.

Beauty read Freud and smoked cigarettes,
Was smart, milk came in bottles, those vessels
Rattled, and genocide was still
Locked in the razor of one ill heart.

The complex mode puts leaves on trees
And summer is a good idea of the mind
Long before ever it was experience –

For we imagine knowledge to be good
And sure, even though, as Eden's children
Mostly what we knew was unconfined –
Our syntax slipped away from land,

Our rocking beds sailed on moonlight
The frost of sky our beaconing horizon.
Awake ghost voyager now, who sank

In the unmoored mind's Mariana,
Unrafted, swollen with brain-rot,
Wracks of passion – unable to know friend
Or pirate in the shadow of shadow.

The sublime may call for clarity
But is often served by vague men who doom
Their jutting prows to strike odd reefs,

Unroofed by calm lingo and straighter goals.
Only in subtle bays or surface shoals
Do tides or pools destroy; not in desert rooms;
The gloom is the sea spray breaking in.

So were your self-made cuts to brow
Of mad projections (of madder maps) both slight
Surface and submarine profound too – sufficient

To render sinking thoughts and feelings
Mirroring out emotion, casting a beam to blind –
Blindness not bestowing wisdom but poison
To fog the clown, whose mask of white pain

Conveys words for pain as well; mascara on skin
That goes to the roots subcutaneous and beyond.
To die alone is to contain a sorrow blossoming

Before sane spring arrives, to know disorder
Thriving like a bulb bled in shaken ground,
Still the ground the only self that one can own,
So one's garden is infested with an early frost even

In the middle of a bright-seeming normal sun.
A renaissance as rain bows down the cherry tree,
As men cough in thin hallways before they frown

To click at keys that lead them on through frail doors
To places of walls, pale carpets and burns on floors
That speak of beige traffic, and fisticuffs in closets.
To fail is obscure – it means one first could win,

Be laurelled, in order to sink, like Satan; you did;
I see this unmastery fight itself off now in me.
Twilight like a courtier bows at the long glass pane;

The Queen of Night allows access to her pavilion.
O, high sensation and archaic claims of style!
The tree that latticed our bodies with light and shade
When we wake is not a metaphor or natural –

Spoken into greenery by this thrill of penmanship –
Spendthrift and untidy on a foolscap before sleep.
Your adoration has slackened on the bed

And yet by force of habit are we both read
On one page forever unioned by a line's crown.
Such a coronation of an abstract love is
Grandiose perfection of the written ring.

THE AILMENT

What got there, got there
then it stayed. *Like glue*
a doctor implied. *Like prayer*
argued another clad like a father
black as grease. It stung
and stuck inside. *A thorn*

she cried; *a hornet having died*
the priest complained – *unsin
thy side!* It was presented
in a finding so I had to decide:
*pull out the fervid pin or wasp
away to little else besides lather*

on a shaved boy's chin. Its clasp
was like wax on a ski or an LP's skin.
It slid about, it grooved, it played
the length and lines of me, a musicness
unto breath. *A tiny ceaseless death*
the dentist opined then wanted cash.

It felt like wine-slosh in my brainpan.
All night I travelled in my bed, a train.
Each carriage disgorged an ailment
but this main thing only grew in size.
It happened finally to emit a claim
on my own name. It wanted out

but as me. I feigned indifference
to my external self, retained some
dignity. Soon though, unguents came
and took the resourceful fluid for a stroll.
It shook off the air and walked upright, so
everyone who saw it nodded at *my soul.*

After the boy band incident

I became afraid of champagne.
Looked up for signs of spit.
No longer Beliebed.
Went in every direction at once.

Was the new kid on a scooter.
Danced to myself.
Heard my heart beat, beat, beat.
My voice was autotuned.

I walked out of sync.
My arms were full of broken dolls.
I ate scandal for breakfast.
I took it, and that, and that too.

I feared five star hotels.
I feared five star windows.
Sniffed tabloid paper for kicks.
I was a page three boy.

The stories I read came true.
I was in a shocker.
Called Simon Simon, Lou Lou.
I was backstreet frontpage.

I was electronic and empty.
I was hand-picked young.
My life went west.
I smelled like a back seat.

My shadow, my entourage.
My sanity was syndicated.
My doctors and lawyers called from LA.
My dry-cleaning was paid for.

My facebook was not my own.
I was blamed for doing too much.
I was hopped up on capital F.
I was not wanted.

I was a report being made.
I woke in the night screaming hits.
I was 2.30 am stumbling out.
Hit an all-time low.

The Fourth King

I could have done more, following that star;
pausing, let my eyes wander, at the oasis, though,
to other, closer flashings. Light on the gold
around a girl's throat. The pomegranate's myriad
redness, interior stars clotted into fruit;

the way that water when it rises from a well
weighs nothing in its sweet necessity. The swell
of her breast as she breathed. Night cold as a blade,
and all the other stars, though never as bright,
strangely alluring in their alternative light.

So, I stayed days and nights among the travellers:
some with tangled slaves; others rich in stories
alone; our opulence was limited by our place
in the desert; we would fast again before winter
had brightened off, as each chose when to leave

this slivered ideal of a paradise, no larger than
a small market in a dusty town; but flourishing
this time in green and moist insouciance, turned
against the blurring white hot outwards at our faces.
Had I known what the others found in that barn

I might not have traded places. Their shy sunburnt
gaze fell upon a tiresome greatness demanding action;
satiated, I stayed put in some small Eden to grow old,
never wondering what the child said or did or knows.

Unfinished Study of a French Girl

Barely there, if at all,
the one that got away,

semi-French,
against the wall,

it's only air where art
could have been; the stroke

of seconds that slip between
what is night, and what

might be a dream.
Maybe she was a student

who never had to pose again;
a doctor's patient never seen.

Half invisible, half known,
barely mysterious, just

browning greys, greens.
A face that happens

to remain, almost a boy –
because to form is to decide

only the name
makes her a girl, and even then,

she looks past that decision.
She looks:

she has a bare face. It is a body
that's undone. Whatever

didn't happen happened
for a reason, or none;

imagination's lost address,
a day the umbrella stayed at home

and wasn't needed
when it failed to rain;

the time the prayer was unsaid
at the graveside

of the passerby in the lane
quick and never dead.

She isn't quite alive,
but that's the same with most paint.

Her being fractional
makes her heart beat fainter;

at least it's possible to hear
her breath out-gathering

like a song one ought to know
but can't quite place

on the mirror she kept in
her purse on the day

she almost came
to Whistler's studio.

On Learning His Godson Has The "Language Gene" Defect FoxP2

Unsinging songbird, love's signals
talon you no tune. The little ring

inside your heart never breaks,
won't know to start. Small wing,

refrain-robbed, your language genes
are a muted branching; unheard, seen –

bright bird, tongueless, young and wild.
Confusion of syllables, lack of spring

upon a surprising note, tender
or offering, means no reason

to hear, as no care extends,
hems you in, away from flight

of singing, that breaks day's stems
when we are woken outright

from dreaming by fowl stylistics,
their unparliamentary delight

in knocking sleep with a beak's baton,
a symphonic rapping of night's lectern.

O my songbird, I will sing for you,
I have this sprightly chance, Alex,

to be the line that runs from your
winged injury to my uncle's tongue.

I'll swoop and dive, roar the glad
sound we wish all songbirds had,

and in your silence key
a dumb way to play your defect

to perfection, as if my lyric vocals
shared across the sky to nephew –

given as love spreads its feathering.
So our duet is true, even if only

unsolo by mechanical virtue;
we break anatomy's musical bonds

unfiring links of dopamine or mind,
to find where upfiring sound can lie

beyond its locked places, song-flight
swanning up as kissing makes union

and larks bend the sky in a risen two
so notes over notes fall out to ascend.

The Best I Can Do

Please don't tickle the urchin, I'm down
Please exacerbate the kiln, I'm down
Please light the tundra, I'm down
Please alert the mastodon, I'm down
Please kindle the vertebrae, I'm down
Please geographically locate, I'm down
Please tendril the obo, I'm down
Please play the pipe-cleaner, I'm down
Please order the zucchini, I'm down
Please butter the platypus, I'm down
Please dust the penumbra, I'm down
Please grapple with logic, I'm down
Please staple the orange, I'm down
Please fling the Listerine, I'm down
Please invent the zero, I'm down
Please sand the biplane, I'm down
Please wrap the sausage, I'm down
Please decorate the grinder, I'm down
Please flood the playschool, I'm down
Please wrangle the horse trader, I'm down
Please lift the ball gown, I'm down
Please pulley the minstrel, I'm down
Please dance the tambourine, I'm down
Please blackout the ashtray, I'm down
Please spin the gargantuan, I'm down
Please speculate on the divine, I'm down
Please spatula the diamond, I'm down
Please deer the mine-field, I'm down
Please forgive the tiptoes, I'm down
Please kiss the impermeable, I'm down
Please layer the tropical, I'm down
Please sunbeam motility, I'm down
Please clown the Humvee, I'm down
Please terminate bathos, I'm down
Please live up to Hercules, I'm down

Please litigate the first frost, I'm down
Please investigate the pollen, I'm down
Please solve Rapunzel, I'm down
Please scatter empty promise, I'm down
Please kettle-bell sweatpants, I'm down
Please listen to me sweetly, I'm down
Please fillet my sweetbread, I'm down
Please levitate my bone shop, I'm down
Please sway my two-tones, I'm down
Please rack my diphthongs, I'm down
Please mascot my tumbleweed, I'm down
Please rocket my lip-gloss, I'm down
Please lock my locket love, I'm down
Please leave the party soon, I'm down
Please part the red leaves, I'm down
Please book the palace, I'm down
Please monopolise the moon, I'm down
Please drive me round and round, I'm down
Please wear shades and salivate, I'm down
Please buy Alaska, I'm down
Please squint the matchstick, I'm down.

In Memoriam, Seamus Heaney

A day after parliament stopped the British from war
and now the heart-stopping news
you are no longer the bearer
of a passport that let you travel far and wide.

Ready to be lugged and thrown, however gently
into the difficult ground you measured
as it was sown, with seed or wound - to flower
only later, for it is near-autumn, and the harvest

coming in is not for you to see or taste.
There will be massacres and weapons inspectors
Sunday, and the year after, and arguably
until time stops working, and it never does.

Only bodies halt, and that is a bitterness
to drink down. Unworded hearts fail. Words go far.

The Book of Platitudes

Because it does not matter
It matters

It says nothing
Which is important

As there is no meaning
It means more

Love is empty
Like the sun is down

I wanted to be great
Then only good

I fear what comes next
Since I fear what was

Let go of the future
And enjoy the past

Dancing is a circle
Open to the sky

Your house is burning
Your water is happy

I come as a man
I come as a woman

When you bury my heart
Do it gently

When you read my poems
Do it with gusto

When you come to kill me
Forget your weapons

Rain is a chandelier
God made for poets

I never saw a tree
That didn't see me first

We are killing the planet
One lie at a time

My soul is named
After your soul

Time is a wheel
It had to be invented

Fire is only angry
When it is cold

I love the wind
When I am running

When my father died
I didn't

The whole world
Is precisely that

Half an apple
Gives you half the knowledge

I left the garden early
And missed my serpent

Slip into your skin
And make me uncomfortable

I am only a song
So sue me

Lyricism is the last escape
Of the failed novelist

Art is only as long
As the bread line

Revolutions turn out to be
Failed romances

History is a long list
Of Historians

These aren't aphorisms
Just poor excuses

I wanted to tell you
Then remembered truth

Don't be kinder
Than you can afford to be

Pay no one's taxes
And everyone's singing lessons

Buy poetry and never
Have to die alone

In my last dream
I was awake

Tonight I am going
To last week

If this was the only kiss
It couldn't be better

Drink and let's go
What is waiting won't

I loved many times
I loved only once with love

What I couldn't do in words
I could do in thought

Whenever I think about it
It doesn't rhyme

I wanted to be good
But ended up as grit

Break the ice
And open winter to the sea

Acknowledgements

Editorial Note: As much as possible we have kept the original British/Canadian spelling where sense allowed, with a few exceptions.

This *Selected Poems* has been selected and edited by the Canadian poet Catherine Graham, and I am particularly grateful to her for her excellent and thoughtful work with me here. In choosing the poems, she drew on a few new or early unpublished poems, and then again, my eight previously published poetry books: *Budavox* (1999), *Cafe Alibi* (2002), *Rue du Regard* (2004), *Winter Tennis* (2007) – all published by DC Books, Montreal; *Seaway: New & Selected* (2008), from Salmon, Ireland; *Mainstream Love Hotel* (2009) from Tall-Lighthouse, UK; as well as the more recent *England Is Mine* (2011) from Punchy Books, and in 2012, *When All My Disappointments Came At Once*, Tightrope Books, Toronto.

These have all been small press collections, and so I am particularly grateful for the care and time their publishers and editors, often poets themselves, took to make them so beautiful to look at, let alone, read: Robert Allen, Steve Luxton, Jessie Lendennie, Jason Camlot, Les Robinson and Halli Villegas, thank you so much. The poems here are the latest, and as far as I imagine, final versions. I also wish to thank Mariela Griffor for being so generous and supportive in letting this book become so long, in letting this book come into being at all.

Over the years, a number of poets and writers (aside from those already named)—often but not always close friends—have worked with me on my poetry, whether in workshops or cafes or by phone, email and letter—and I want to thank them here: Alfred Corn; Charles Bernstein; Denise Riley; Emily Berry; Eric Ormsby; Gary Geddes; George Szirtes; James Byrne; Karen Wortley; Kathryn Maris; Kevin Higgins; Lachlan Mackinnon; Lisa Pasold; Patrick Chapman; Sandeep Parmar; Tom Walsh;Mark Ford and Zoe Brigley Thompson. Other friends and colleagues—often poets—have been kind and supportive along the way, such as Andrew Motion, Clive Scott, Regie Cabico, Don Share, Dr E. Sass, Luke Kennard, Martin Mooney, Martin Penny, Fr. Oliver Brennan, Thor Bishopric, Bridget Hourican and Wendy Cope.

A special thanks to Ann Kitz at the Colville Estate, and Felicia Cukier at the Art Gallery of Ontario, for being so helpful in my quest to have a great work of art on the cover of this book.

Finally, I wish to name those members of my family who, from when I was young, most encouraged me to become a poet: my mother Margaret, my aunt and uncle Bev and Jack Swift, and my grandmother, Melita Hume. No one in my life has been a more constant source of love and support, however, than my beautiful, kind and very brilliant wife, Sara, whose unique balance of creativity, good humour, style and energy has been my rock.

About the Book

Todd Swift has an entry in the *Oxford Companion to Modern Poetry in English* (second edition, 2013), which seeks to list the most influential poets of the last 100 years. Over the past three decades Swift has established himself as one of the most international, stylish, and generous, of poet-editors now at work in the English language. His poetry has been almost unique in combining equal measures of erudition and emotionality, modern rhetoric and postmodern pastiche, experiment and lyricism. Swift's formal virtuosity, sense of poetic artifice and love of word play is constantly challenged by the desire to also sincerely explore (if not express), issues of the body and soul: desire, rage, fear, and loss of faith.

Swift has written these poems while living in Montreal, Budapest, Paris and London. Whether charting the anguish of male infertility and its impact on a marriage, or the joys of lovemaking; the austerities of religious belief and the anxieties of childhood; the romance and realities of travel and homesickness – the enriching fecundity of language always, ultimately, redeems the sickness at the heart of the rose. Drawing on his previous 8 collections, published in Canada, Ireland and Great Britain, Swift's *The Ministry of Emergency Situations: Selected Poems* is a milestone, allowing American readers, for the first time, to see in broad view, the whole of his large poetic oeuvre.

CPSIA information can be obtained
at www.ICGtesting.com
Printed in the USA
FFOW03n1801020315
11437FF